Contents

The authors

Richard White is a partner in a London solicitor's practice, and he has been working with the law relating to children since 1969. He qualified in 1971. He is legal adviser to a number of adoption agencies and Chair of the Special Educational Needs and Disability Tribunal.

Anthony Harbour was admitted as a solicitor in 1980. He is a partner in a London solicitor's practice, where he specialises in health and social service law. He is a legal member of the Mental Health Review Tribunal and the Family Health Service Appeal Authority.

Richard Williams is Professor of Mental Health Strategy in the University of Glamorgan and a consultant child and adolescent psychiatrist in Gwent Healthcare NHS Trust. He is also Chair of the Academy of Medical Royal Colleges in Wales, Chairman of the Welsh Division of the Royal College of Psychiatrists and Director of Conferences at the Royal College of Psychiatrists.

Edited by Richard Williams

SAFEGUARDS FOR YOUNG MINDS

Young People and Protective Legislation

SECOND EDITION

Richard White, Anthony Harbour
and Richard Williams

Gaskell is an imprint of the Royal College of Psychiatrists,
17 Belgrave Square, London SW1X 8PG
http://www.rcpsych.ac.uk

British Library Cataloguing-in-Publication Data

A catalogue record for this book is available from the British Library

ISBN 1 904671 02 0

The Royal College of Psychiatrists is a registered charity (no. 228636).

Printed in Cromwell Press Ltd, Trowbridge, UK

Preface

This book is aimed at all practitioners who work with children and young people. We consider it vital that all these professionals should be well acquainted with the legal, ethical and moral principles that underpin their practice. They should clearly understand the components of lawfully valid consent, how it should be obtained, and possible avenues of approach to those challenging situations when consent is withheld or withdrawn, or when the child or young person lacks the capacity to give consent. Acting in the best interests of children and young people also brings duties and responsibilities, and practitioners need to be familiar with those that are spelled out in law. This text explains the domain of the law as it applies in England and Wales in late 2003.

We, the authors, are aware from our practice and teaching of the value that professionals from all relevant disciplines put on being offered opportunities to talk through both the decisions they make and those on which they are asked to advise. We hope that this book will provide a framework for these kinds of reflective learning and practice.

Colleagues frequently tell us that there are problems in the law when its strictures do not cover adequately the realities of professional practice in an evidence-based world, which is encouraging greater user and carer involvement and much more frequent questioning of professionals' decisions. Our experience is that many concerns are dispelled by greater familiarity with the contents of the various legislative frameworks and opportunities to work through hypothetical cases.

This book summarises many of the key pieces of legislation that affect professional child care and treatment practice. Our intention is to meet the needs of trainees in a variety of disciplines as well to provide an aide-memoire for busy practitioners who have completed their formal training. Additionally, we have been asked to put into print key extracts from the notes for the section 12(2) training courses that were prepared for the Royal College of Psychiatrists by Anthony Harbour. Consequently, we hope that children's practitioners who are training to be section 12(2) approved doctors or approved social workers (ASWs) will also find this book helpful.

None of the contents can replace experience, but our hope is that this book will act as a primer and as an entry point to more detailed information. This is why we have referred in the text to many points of law, the relevant Acts and statutory instruments and to cases heard before Courts of Record. Additionally, we provide a full and updated bibliography.

Origins of this text

In 1992, the Royal College of Psychiatrists published the *Concise Guide to the Children Act 1989*. That slim volume was highly successful and very popular. We (Richard Williams and Richard White) were asked to edit a second edition. We decided not just to review, check and update the *Concise Guide*, but to develop a new text from the original volume. The new title, which we have retained, marked the broader scope of the new text.

At the time that *Safeguards for Young Minds* was first published, a new edition of the Code of Practice to the Mental Health Act 1983 was overdue and so the text contained warnings about the continuing legal accuracy of some paragraphs in the then current Code. Subsequently, a new Code was published and this alone requires us to update our book. In 2001, 2002 and 2003, the Royal College of Psychiatrists developed, tested and ran courses for child and adolescent psychiatrists who aspired to be approved under section 12(2) of the Mental Health Act 1983. They were highly successful and well-rated by participants. Consequently, the editor of this volume agreed to incorporate rather more about consent, mental health legislation and the Code of Practice in this revised and updated edition.

You may ask why we are publishing a second edition when current mental health legislation in England and Wales is being reviewed. The answer lies in the rising number of requests for advice and training at a time when there is considerable uncertainty about when any new Mental Health Bill will be put before Parliament, enacted, and then implemented.

We perceive that the rush to learn about the Children Act 1989 soon after its passage through Parliament has now slowed. Perhaps paradoxically, many doctors in postgraduate training receive less teaching on, and assistance with the Children Act 1989 than was the case a decade ago. Additionally, the rise of clinical governance and greater awareness of the importance of involving children and families in all aspects of service commissioning and delivery has brought fresh concentration on the nature of lawfully valid consent and requests for advice about it. We think that these influences link with the recent popularity of courses offering training on the relevant legislation and the many enquiries for advice that each of us receives.

Since the first edition of *Safeguards for Young Minds* was published, there has been a number of important changes in the law. The Human Rights Act became law in 1998. While the Children Act 1989 and Mental Health Act 1983 are substantially 'Human Rights Act compliant', it is important for practitioners to be aware of its contents and the implications of that Act for practice based on other legislative frameworks.

The Children (Leaving Care) Act received Royal Assent in 2000. That legislation amended the Children Act 1989 so as to impose a duty on local authorities looking after children to advise, assist and befriend them (for extended periods in some cases) after they leave care. More recent still is the Adoption and Children Act 2002. This updated second edition of *Safeguards for Young Minds* provides information on certain of the significant changes consequent on each of these new Acts.

Furthermore, time has elapsed since the Children Act 1989 was implemented. Changes through common or case law continue to be made.

Practitioners should be aware of the changes to the original statute that have resulted from decisions made in Courts of Record. We have updated our text to reflect all pertinent changes to the Children Act up to the spring of 2003.

Taking into account all of these circumstances, we think the time is right to bring forward a new edition.

It is appropriate to begin by quoting from the foreword to the Concise Guide:

> 'This volume summarises the major changes in the law in England and Wales which took place when the Children Act 1989 received Royal Assent. ... One of the consequences of the Act has been to bring together much of the law relating to children, in England and Wales, in a single statute. This is a substantial achievement. The position of children in law has been enhanced and a range of new orders drawn up. The Royal College of Psychiatrists perceived that the changes were such that they would require all professional staff who work with children and families to familiarise themselves with the new concepts and the detailed changes will clearly have a significant impact on the work of a great many psychiatrists.'

In summary, we have retained the original purpose of our first book, and therefore updated our survey of the contents of the Children Act 1989 and added much new material relating to application of mental health legislation and the Human Rights Act 1998 in England and Wales.

This new edition

This book is concerned with aspects of the law as it applies to the welfare and protection of minors. In particular, it considers the implications for practitioners of:

- the Human Rights Act 1998;
- the Children Act 1989;
- the Mental Health Act 1983;
- the current Code of Practice to the Mental Health Act, which was laid before Parliament on 3 December 1998 and came into force on 1 April 1999;
- the Mental Health (Patients in the Community) Act 1995;
- the Education Act 1996 and its Code of Practice on Special Educational Needs (2001);
- the Children (Leaving Care) Act 2000, which amends the after-care provisions of the Children Act 1989; and
- certain amendments to the Children Act 1989 made by the Adoption and Children Act 2002.

This book begins with a brief summary of key provisions in the Human Rights Act 1998. It continues with a concise summary of the main provisions of the Children Act 1989 laid out in a popular style which makes relevant information accessible to busy practitioners.

The Mental Health Act 1983 has no lower limit of age for most of its provisions and it therefore applies to minors as well as adults. In this book, we consider particular issues relating to the contents and use of this legislation with younger people.

As in previous editions, we have followed the legal and parliamentary convention of using male pronouns only when we quote from the law, which is written in this manner.

Contents

The original *Concise Guide* consisted of 11 chapters. The first edition of *Safeguards for Young Minds*, and this enlarged second edition, consists of 15 chapters as well as an extensive bibliography; this second edition is also the first edition to be fully indexed. Chapter 1 overviews the Human Rights Act 1998 and the core contents of the Children Act 1989 are summarised in Chapters 2 to 5. In response to the requests that we have received, Chapter 6 draws on a variety of legislative frameworks to provide a more substantial commentary on matters relating to valid consent to treatment. That chapter deals with matters that are of recurrent concern to practitioners including, for example, a section on consent to a service for people who misuse substances.

Chapter 7 leads a sequence of five chapters that are concerned with the legal mechanisms for resolving situations in which it might be considered by practitioners that some form of admission of a minor to hospital or other facility is required, occasionally with compulsion. Chapter 7 deals with informal admission and summarises the implications of legislation for the conduct of children's care in hospital. The next two chapters concern restriction of liberty: Chapter 8 summarises the statutory basis provided by the Children Act 1989; Chapter 9 deals with the provisions of the Mental Health Act 1983 and its current Code of Practice (which, it should be noted, has a chapter (31) about children and young people) much more substantially than was the case in the previous edition. Thus, we recognise that practitioners find this subject confusing and provocative of anxiety and concern.

We also recognise the tensions that arise for individual practitioners who try to work within and apply the law appropriately. In particular, we note the uncertainty expressed by legal, health care and child care colleagues about when to use procedures provided by the Children Act 1989 in preference to those provided by the Mental Health Act 1983, and vice versa. To clarify these and other issues, Chapter 10 offers our interpretation and advice rather than simple reiteration of the law. In advising on the occasions and circumstances when clinical practitioners should adopt the provisions of a particular Act, we set out a series of factors and pointers that might be applied to test each circumstance with a view to aid them to find the best and most appropriate way forward.

Chapter 11 includes a commentary on the effects of the various legislations on children's placements, after-care and their entitlement to mental health services. Chapter 12 overviews wardship and the inherent jurisdiction of the High Court, which still remain available. Chapter 13 summarises the impact of the Education Act 1996 as it relates to special educational needs and the rights of children and their parents in this respect. Chapter 14 summarises the complaints procedures that arise from several legislative frameworks. We hope that the revised and updated information in Chapter 15 relating to work in the courts and the position of expert witnesses will prove helpful. Finally, we have updated the bibliography and included for the first time a number of internet sources of further information.

We hope that this new volume will be as helpful as its predecessors in interpreting the current legal position not only for psychiatrists but also for children's practitioners, teachers, and health care and local authority managers.

Legal advice

We think that it is important that all agencies, their managers and individual professionals involved in delivering services for children and young people should have access to good legal advice. Any general advice in this text cannot replace that. Experience has shown that the opportunity for practitioners and managers to develop relationships with legal practitioners that allow complex legal matters to be explored over time and in relationship to various cases will benefit not only the practitioners themselves but also the children and young people in their care. We strongly support the view that legal advice of this kind is invaluable when it is consistently and reliably available.

Acknowledgements

We acknowledge the enormous help and assistance that we have had from colleagues. One of the authors, Richard White, has undertaken most of the detailed work involved in reviewing the chapters relating to the Children Act 1989. In the last edition, William Bingley provided brief contributions on the Mental Health Act 1989. We take this opportunity to thank William and to acknowledge his contribution to the first edition. Anthony Harbour contributed a section on choosing between the legislative frameworks. In the light of our experience and to reflect requests from others, we have expanded considerably the contents relating to the Mental Health Act 1983. Fortunately, we had been working closely with Anthony Harbour when we received the request for this new edition. He has provided much new material on the Mental Health Act and written the overview of the Human Rights Act 1998.

We also acknowledge with gratitude the contribution made by Julian Beezhold. Dr Beezehold researched and created the flow diagram relating to consent given by or on behalf of children and young people that appears, as Figure 6.2, on pages 64–65. We are grateful to him for allowing us to use the diagram this book.

The original *Concise Guide to the Children Act* drew upon the work of a number of others who provided material directly, provided questions from their own experience that we set out to try to answer or acted as sources of expertise in our formal and informal reflections with them. That process has continued. So, we pay tribute to the advice, friendship and support of Sue Bailey, Ann Gath, Martyn Gay, Judith Glancy, Jean Harris Hendriks, David Jones, Caroline Lindsey, Greg Richardson, Mike Shaw and Mike Shooter, with whom we have had the pleasure of working closely.

1
An overview of the Human Rights Act 1998

Children's rights need to be understood in both a national and an international context. This chapter concentrates on the Human Rights Act 1998. That Act does not, however, deal specifically with children. The key international instrument that does so is the United Nations Convention on the Rights of the Child (CRC), which was ratified by the United Kingdom in 1991. The reason that this book focuses on the Human Rights Act rather than on the CRC is that although the CRC is a comprehensive children's rights code, it cannot be directly enforced in the UK.

The Human Rights Act incorporates the rights and freedoms set out in the European Convention on Human Rights (the Convention) into UK law. It applies in England, Northern Ireland, Scotland and Wales. In this chapter, we use the term 'Convention' to refer to the European Convention and the Human Rights Act, not to the CRC.

Any person who is involved in mental health services, be they policymaker, commissioner, user, carer or professional is affected by the Act. Section 1 states that 'It is unlawful for a public authority to act in a way which is incompatible with a Convention Right.' 'Public authority' is very widely defined, to include courts, and also 'any person certain of whose functions are functions of a public nature'.

This section of the Act means that agencies and professionals who work with children are required to act in ways that recognise the basic human rights of all the children under their care.

The rights protected under the Human Rights Act 1998 include:

- the right to life (Article 2)
- protection from torture and inhuman or degrading treatment or punishment (Article 3)
- protection from slavery and forced or compulsory labour (Article 4)
- the right to liberty and security of person (Article 5)
- the right to fair trial (Article 6)
- protection from retrospective criminal offences (Article 7)
- the protection of private and family life (Article 8)

- freedom of thought and conscience and religion (Article 9)
- freedom of association and assembly (Article 11)
- the right to marry and found a family (Article 12)
- freedom from discrimination (Article 14).

Most relevant articles

In this paragraph, we consider in more detail the articles most likely to be relevant to children and young people.

Article 3

No one shall be subjected to torture or to inhuman or degrading treatment or punishment.

Article 5

1. Everyone has the right to liberty and security of person. No one shall be deprived of his liberty save in the following cases and in accordance with a procedure prescribed by law:
    a. the lawful detention of a person after conviction by a competent court;
    b. the lawful arrest or detention of a person for non-compliance with the lawful order of a court or in order to secure the fulfilment of any obligation prescribed by law;
    c. the lawful arrest or detention of a person effected for the purpose of bringing him before the competent legal authority on reasonable suspicion of having committed an offence or when it is reasonably considered necessary to prevent his committing an offence or fleeing after having done so;
    d. the detention of a minor by lawful order for the purpose of educational supervision or his lawful detention for the purpose of bringing him before the competent legal authority;
    e. the lawful detention of persons for the prevention of the spreading of infectious diseases, of persons of unsound mind, alcoholics or drug addicts or vagrants;
    f. the lawful arrest or detention of a person to prevent his effecting an unauthorised entry into the country or of a person against whom action is being taken with a view to deportation or extradition.
2. Everyone who is arrested shall be informed promptly, in a language which he understands, of the reasons for his arrest and of any charge against him.
3. Everyone arrested or detained in accordance with the provisions of paragraph 1.c. of this article shall be brought promptly before a judge or

other officer authorised by law to exercise judicial power and shall be entitled to trial within a reasonable time or to release pending trial. Release may be conditioned by guarantees to appear for trial.

4. Everyone who is deprived of his liberty by arrest or detention shall be entitled to take proceedings by which the lawfulness of his detention shall be decided speedily by a court and his release ordered if the detention is not lawful.
5. Everyone who has been the victim of arrest or detention in contravention of the provisions of this article shall have an enforceable right to compensation.

Article 6

1. In the determination of his civil rights and obligations or of any criminal charge against him, everyone is entitled to a fair and public hearing within a reasonable time by an independent and impartial tribunal established by law. Judgment shall be pronounced publicly but the press and public may be excluded from all or part of the trial in the interests of morals, public order or national security in a democratic society, where the interests of juveniles or the protection of the private life of the parties so require, or to the extent strictly necessary in the opinion of the court in special circumstances where publicity would prejudice the interests of justice.
2. Everyone charged with a criminal offence shall be presumed innocent until proved guilty according to law.
3. Everyone charged with a criminal offence has the following minimum rights:
   a. to be informed promptly, in a language which he understands and in detail, of the nature and cause of the accusation against him;
   b. to have adequate time and facilities for the preparation of his defence;
   c. to defend himself in person or through legal assistance of his own choosing or, if he has not sufficient means to pay for legal assistance, to be given it free when the interests of justice so require;
   d. to examine or have examined witnesses against him and to obtain the attendance and examination of witnesses on his behalf under the same conditions as witnesses against him;
   e. to have the free assistance of an interpreter if he cannot understand or speak the language used in court.

Article 8

1. Everyone has the right to respect for his private and family life, his home and his correspondence.
2. There shall be no interference by a public authority with the exercise of this right except such as is in accordance with the law and is necessary in a democratic society in the interests of national security, public safety or the economic well-being of the country, for the prevention of disorder or crime, for the protection of health or morals, or for the protection of the rights and freedoms of others.

Implications for the health care and welfare professions

The new language of human rights is an important development, but it does not threaten existing standards of good practice. This is because the 'Convention Rights' are not usually absolute rights, and it is possible to balance different rights against each other. For example, a parent's right to make decisions must be balanced against the child's own rights to privacy, and the need to protect the child's health. Similarly, the child's right to liberty is not absolute.

The articles that are most relevant to children who are being treated against their will, either under the Mental Health Act or with the agreement of a person with parental responsibility, are Article 5, which provides the right to liberty and security, and Article 8, which provides the right to respect for private and family life.

The Human Rights Act should be regarded as a human rights code that is complementary to existing statute and common law. For example, if a child is being treated against their wishes outside the Mental Health Act, their rights given by Article 5 must be considered alongside that of a parent to seek medical treatment on the child's behalf given by Article 8 (for example, *Nielsen v. Denmark* [1998] 11 EHRR 175).

Guidance from the British Medical Association (BMA) in 2001 suggests that the Human Rights Act will require reconsideration of the power of parents to authorise the compulsory treatment of children:

> '... while uncertainty remains regarding the extent to which practice will change in relation to minors' rights as a result of the Human Rights Act, such rights are increasingly seen as an important matter for debate and re-evaluation ... It is conceivable therefore that as we become more accustomed to looking at a range of issues, such as health care, through the prism of human rights, views about parental authority over competent children will also undergo significant changes' (British Medical Association, 2001).

2
An overview of the Children Act 1989

The Children Act 1989, implemented for the most part on 14 October 1991, introduced comprehensive changes to legislation in England and Wales affecting the welfare of children. The Act:

- reinforces the autonomy of families through definition of parental responsibility;
- provides for support from local authorities, in particular for families whose children are in need; and
- legislates to protect children who may be suffering or are likely to suffer significant harm.

Annual reports on the progress of the Act were published by the Children Act Advisory Committee until 1997, but the Committee was then abolished. The Government is required to publish a report on the Act every 5 years, and statistics on its application are also available. There are also research reports on the operation of the Act (see Aldgate & Statham, 2001).

Aims of the Act

The main aims of the Act are:

- to bring together private and public law in one framework;
- to achieve a better balance between protecting children and enabling parents to challenge state intervention;
- to encourage greater partnership between statutory authorities and parents;
- to promote the use of voluntary arrangements;
- to restructure the framework of the courts to facilitate management of family proceedings.

Principles of the Act

The main principles and provisions embodied in this legislation are that:

- the welfare of children must be the paramount consideration when the courts are making decisions about them;
- the concept of parental responsibility has replaced that of parental rights;
- children have the ability to be parties, separate from their parents, in legal proceedings;
- local authorities are charged with duties to identify children in need and to safeguard and promote their welfare;
- certain duties and powers are conferred upon local authorities to provide services for children and families;
- a checklist of factors must be considered by the courts before reaching decisions;
- orders under this Act should not be made unless it can be shown that this is better for the child than not making an order;
- delay in deciding questions concerning children is likely to prejudice their welfare.

Scope and contents of the Act

The scope of the Act is extremely wide. Consequently, it has major implications for the practice of all who work with or for children. It changed the standing of children and young people in law, introduced new concepts relating to the responsibilities of adults, changed the structure and functioning of the courts, and provided an entirely new range of orders in both private and public law relating to the care of children.

The Act is arranged in 12 Parts and 15 Schedules. Particular attention is drawn to Part I which establishes its core concepts.

Part I Introductory
This part establishes the principle of law that the welfare of children is of paramount importance and the concept of parental responsibility.

Part II Orders with respect of children in family proceedings
Part II establishes a range of orders known as 'section 8 orders'.

Part III Local authority support for children and families (and Schedule 2)
This part lays upon each local authority a range of duties and powers relating to providing services for children and their families. In particular, it details the law in relationship to the provision of accommodation for children by local authorities and establishes the concept of children being *looked after* by the local authorities.

Part IV Care and supervision
Part IV deals with the provisions concerning care and supervision orders and establishes the threshold criteria (see pages 29–32) that must be satisfied before a court can make one of these orders.

Part V Protection of children
Part V deals with child assessment and emergency protection orders and with police protection.

Part VI Community homes

Part VII Voluntary Homes and voluntary organisations

Part VIII Registered children's homes
Since April 2002, this Part has been replaced by provisions in the Care Standards Act 2000.

Part IX Private arrangements for fostering children

Part X Childminding and day care for young children
Since April 2002, this Part has been replaced by provisions in the Care Standards Act 2000.

Part XI The Secretary of State's supervisory functions and responsibilities

Part XII Miscellaneous and general

Key concepts in the Children Act 1989

Parental responsibility

A central change introduced by the Children Act 1989 was substitution of the concept of parental responsibility for that of parental rights. The Act defines parental responsibility as 'all the rights, duties, powers, responsibilities and authority which by law a parent of a child has in relation to the child and his property': s3(1).

Parental responsibility is given to both the child's father and mother where they are married to each other at, or after, the child's conception. In the case of unmarried parents, the mother has parental responsibility and the father does not have parental responsibility for his child unless he acquires it. This is achieved by the father's successful application to a court or when the father and mother make between them a parental responsibility agreement or (when the relevant provisions of the Adoption and Children Act 2002 are implemented) if the father's name is on the child's birth certificate. A guardian who is appointed by the court or by a parent also acquires parental responsibility on taking up appointment: s5.

More than one person may have parental responsibility for the same child at the same time. Any person who has parental responsibility does not cease to have that duty solely because some other person subsequently acquires parental responsibility. In brief, parental responsibility is something that parents have and, short of adoption (or freeing for adoption), do not lose.

Welfare of the child

When a court determines a question with respect to the upbringing of a child, the child's welfare shall be the court's paramount consideration. Two additional points concerning the welfare of such a child need to be considered.

First, the courts are required, in public and private law proceedings, to establish a timetable and give directions for the expeditious handling of each case, because the courts must have regard to the general principle that any delay is likely to prejudice the welfare of the child: s1(2). This is not intended to be rigid. Purposeful delay, as opposed to unplanned drift, is acceptable (*C v. Solihull Metropolitan Borough Council* [1993] 1 FLR 290).

Second, courts must have regard, in opposed applications for a section 8 order and in care proceedings to a checklist concerning the child's circumstances as set out in section 1(3). This list of matters concerns:

- the ascertainable wishes and feelings of the child (considered in the light of his age and understanding);
- his physical, emotional and educational needs;
- the likely effect on him of any change in his circumstances;
- his age, sex, background and any characteristics of his which the court considers relevant;
- any harm that he has suffered or is at risk of suffering (for definition of harm, see page 30);
- how capable each of his parents, and any other person in relation to whom the court considers the question to be relevant, is of meeting his needs; and
- the range of powers available to the court in the proceedings in question.

A wider list of matters relating to circumstances in which adoption is being considered is contained in the Adoption and Children Act 2002.

These lists are known as the 'welfare checklists'.

Partnership and cooperation

The major changes in law relating to children that resulted from the Children Act 1989 have their most significant effect upon:

- parents;
- others having responsibilities for children;
- local authorities (see Department of Health, 1995*a*).

Nonetheless, the Act has substantial implications for the National Health Service (NHS) and for all health care professionals and managers who come into contact with children.

One of the main themes of the Children Act 1989 is encouragement of greater cooperation between those responsible for children and statutory or voluntary agencies. Section 27 enables local authorities to request the help of any other authority or person, including health authorities, in relationship to specified actions. Those so requested must comply if the request is compatible with their own statutory duties and obligations and does not unduly prejudice the discharge of any of their functions. At least 18 sections of the Act have implications for strategic health authorities, local health boards, primary care trusts, NHS trusts and for health services staff generally. An editorial review by Williams & Salmon (2002) examines the blocks to effective collaboration and potential resolutions to them.

In the 1980s the government published *Working Together: A Guide to Arrangements for Inter-agency Cooperation for the Protection of Children from Abuse*. A second edition was published in October 1991 (Home Office *et al*, 1991). The current, third, edition called *Working Together to Safeguard Children: A Guide for Inter-Agency Working to Safeguard and Promote the Welfare of Children* was published in England in 1999 and in Wales in 2001 (Department of Health *et al*, 2000; National Assembly for Wales, 2001*a*). See also *Child Protection: Medical Responsibilities* (Department of Health, 1995*d*), an addendum to *Working Together*, and *Safeguarding Children in Whom Illness is Fabricated or Induced* (Department of Health, 2002).

Local authority services

Part III of the Children Act gives powers and duties to local authorities to provide services for children and their families. Services for children in need and disabled children are brought under one statute. Under Part III, local authorities are required to produce plans setting out their provision of children's services. Strategic health authorities, local health boards, primary care trusts and NHS trusts should be consulted in this process. When assessing the needs of children and families, local authorities will be guided by the *Framework for the Assessment of Children in Need and their Families* (Department of Health, 2000*a*; National Assembly for Wales, 2001*b*) and *Assessing Children in Need and their Families: Practice Guidance* (Department of Health, 2000*b*).

Children in need

A general duty is placed on local authorities to safeguard and promote the welfare of children in their area who are in need and (so far as is consistent with that duty) to promote the upbringing of such children by their families by providing a range and level of services appropriate to those children's needs: s17(1). A child is in need if he is unlikely to achieve or maintain, or to have the opportunity of achieving or maintaining, a reasonable standard of health or development without the provision of services by a local authority under Part III. Equally, he is in need if his health or development is likely to be significantly impaired or further impaired without the provision of such services, or if he is disabled: s17(10, 11). Additional financial systems are in place for children with disabilities: s17A.

Children in local authority accommodation

Local authorities have a duty to provide accommodation for certain children in need: s20(1). An authority may not provide accommodation if any person with parental responsibility for the child, who is willing and able to provide or arrange accommodation, objects to the authority providing it. Unless another person has a residence order, any person who has parental responsibility may remove the child at any time: s20(7). Local authorities should make agreements in writing with parents or other persons with parental responsibility about the service to be provided, if possible before the service is provided (see the Arrangements for Placement of Children (General) Regulations 1991).

Each local authority has duties to the children it looks after (i.e. children accommodated or in care) under sections 23 and 24 of the Children Act. These require the local authority to:

- safeguard and promote their welfare and to make such services available for children cared for by their own parents as appears to the authority reasonable in the case of each particular child;
- ascertain, as far as practicable, the wishes and feelings of the child, his parents, any other person who has parental responsibility and any other person the authority considers to be relevant, before making any decision with respect to a child they look after or propose to look after;
- give due consideration, having regard to his age and understanding, to such wishes and feelings of the child as they have been able to ascertain and to his religious persuasion, racial origin and cultural and linguistic background;
- consider the wishes and feelings of any person mentioned above;
- advise, assist and befriend each child with a view to promoting his welfare when he ceases to be in the local authority's care; and
- provide advice and assistance to qualifying persons between 16 years and 21 years old.

An authority looking after a child must, by section 23(2), provide him with accommodation while he is in care, and must:

- maintain him in a children's home (Children's Homes Regulations 2001);
- maintain him in the care of his family, relative or other suitable person (Fostering Services Regulations 2002);

- maintain him in the care of a parent or person who has parental responsibility (Accommodation of Children with Parents Regulations 1991); or
- make other appropriate arrangements which comply with such regulations.

As far as is reasonably practicable and consistent with the child's welfare (s23(7) and (8)):

- accommodation should be near the child's home;
- accommodation for a disabled child should not be unsuitable to his needs; and
- siblings should be accommodated together.

The duty of local authorities in respect of rehabilitation

An authority must make arrangements to enable a child to live with his family unless this is not practical or consistent with his welfare. If he is in care, he may only be placed with parents, or a person with parental responsibility, under strictly controlled conditions: s23.

Case reviews and complaints procedures

Under section 26 of the Children Act, the local authority is required to review the case of each child it looks after, at regular intervals, in accordance with the Review of Children's Cases Regulations 1991.

Where a child is being looked after by a local authority, accommodated on a local authority's behalf by a voluntary organisation or otherwise accommodated in a registered children's home, he will be entitled to use the complaints procedure, also required by section 26 and established in accordance with the Representations Procedure (Children) Regulations 1991. Under sections 24D and 26, local authorities must establish and publicise their procedures for considering any representations, including complaints, made by:

- a child who they are looking after or who is not being looked after but is in need;
- a person who qualifies for after-care services (see Chapter 11);
- a parent or other person with parental responsibility;
- any foster parent; and
- any other person who the authority or voluntary organisation considers has a sufficient interest in the child's welfare to warrant representations being considered by them about the discharge by the authority or voluntary organisation of any of their functions under Part III in relation to the child.

The procedure must ensure that at least one person, who is not a member or officer of the authority, takes part in the consideration of the complaint and in any discussions held by the authority about the action to be taken in relation to the child in the light of the complaint. The authority must have due regard to the findings of those considering the representation and must notify:

- the child,
- the person making the representation, and
- other affected persons

of the reasons for its decision and of any action taken or to be taken.

While the decision about the child remains with the authority, it may be subject to judicial review if the authority ignores findings or fails to give any satisfactory reasons for its decision.

Further information on complaints procedures is summarised in Chapter 14.

An overview of the orders in the Children Act 1989

	Children Act 1989	Previous legislation
Private Law Orders	Section 8 orders: residence, contact, specific issue, and prohibited steps orders	Custody, care and control, and access orders
Public Law Orders	Care, supervision, and education supervision orders Secure accommodation	Care and supervision orders Secure accommodation
Orders for the Protection of Children	Child assessment, emergency protection, and police protection orders	Place of safety order
Wardship	No longer to be used by local authorities as a route into care, but orders under the inherent jurisdiction of the High Court with or without wardship may be available under s100, except that a child may not be both a ward of court and in care	Often used to gain the direction of the court when an application for a care order had failed, was not appropriate, or the result was uncertain

3

Private law orders in the Children Act 1989

Part II of the Children Act 1989 made major changes in the orders available in family proceedings in which questions arise concerning the welfare of children. The concepts of custody, care and control, and access, which had previously caused confusion and misunderstanding, were swept away to be replaced by a range of new provisions.

The most important of the private law orders are known as 'section 8 orders'. They are:

- the residence order
- the contact order
- the specific issue order
- the prohibited steps order.

Section 8 orders can be made in care proceedings, whether or not the threshold criteria (see pages 29–32) are satisfied, but they cannot be in force at the same time as a care order.

Section 8: Residence Order

Definition

An order settling the arrangements to be made with respect to the person with whom a child is to live.

Qualifying criteria

- A section 8 order can be applied for separately or as part of other proceedings.
- The court is empowered to make a residence order in any family proceedings.
- No court can make a residence order that is to have effect beyond the child's sixteenth birthday unless it is satisfied that the circumstances of the case are exceptional, in which case it may continue until the child reaches the age of 18 years: s9(6).
- A residence order can be made even if the child is in local authority care, but the care order is then discharged: s91(1).

Powers and duties under the order

- A residence order automatically gives the person in whose favour it is made parental responsibility for the child: s12(2).
- When a residence order is in force, no person may either change the child's surname or remove him from the UK without the written consent of every person who has parental responsibility for the child, or without leave of the court: s13(1).
- A person in whose favour there is a residence order may remove the child for any period less than 1 month: s13(2).
- The court can make an order:
    - containing directions as to how it is to be put into effect;
    - imposing conditions that must be complied with by any person in whose favour the order is made, who is a parent or has parental responsibility, or with whom the child is living and to whom the conditions are expressed to apply;
    - to have effect for a specified period, or containing provisions that are to have effect for a specified period; or
    - with 'such incidental, supplemental or consequential provision as the court thinks fit': s11(7).

Application of general principles

- The child's welfare shall be the court's paramount consideration: s1(1).
- Delay is likely to prejudice the welfare of the child: s1(2).

- There is a presumption of no order unless the court considers that to make an order would be better for the child: s1(5).
- The welfare checklist (see page 8) applies (if the application is opposed): s1(4).

Who can apply?

There are two categories of applicant: those who can apply as of right and those who require the leave of the court.

As of right

Section 10(5) provides a right of application to any parent, including:

- the unmarried father;
- a guardian;
- any person who has a residence order;

- any party to a marriage, if the child is a child of the family;
- any person with whom the child has been living for at least 3 years;
- a person who has the consent of each person who has a residence order;
- the local authority, if the child is in care;
- or, in any other case, each person who has parental responsibility.

With leave

- Anyone else, including the child.
- In the case of a local authority foster-parent, then, unless he is a relative of the child or the child has been living with him for 3 years or, after implementation of the Adoption and Children Act 2002, the child has lived with him for a period of at least 1 year immediately preceding the application, he must have the consent of the local authority to apply for the court's leave: s9(3).
- For criteria for granting leave, see section 10(8) and (9).
- The court is able to make a section 8 order on its own motion; that is, without an application being made: s10(1)(b).

Exclusions

A local authority may not apply for a residence order: s9(2).

Respondents/notice

As provided in the Family Proceedings Rules 1991 and the Family Proceedings Courts (Children Act 1989) Rules 1991.

Venue

Magistrates' court, county court or High Court, although this may be limited by a legal aid certificate.

Duration

A residence order ceases to have effect:

- if the parents live together for a continuous period exceeding 6 months: s11(5);
- when the child reaches the age of 16 years or, in exceptional circumstances, 18 years: s91(10).

Appeal

To the High Court from the magistrates' court, and to the Court of Appeal from the county court or High Court.

Variation and discharge

- Any person entitled to apply for a residence order can apply for its variation or discharge.
- Anyone else shall be entitled to do so if the order was made on his application: s10(6).
- The order is discharged by a care order: s91(2).

Section 8: Contact Order

Definition

An order requiring the person with whom a child lives, or is to live, to allow the child to visit or stay with the person named in the order, or for that person and the child otherwise to have contact with each other.

Qualifying criteria

- A section 8 order can be applied for separately or as part of other proceedings.
- The court is empowered to make a contact order in any family proceedings.
- No court can make a residence order that is to have effect beyond the child's sixteenth birthday unless it is satisfied that the circumstances of the case are exceptional, in which case it may continue until the child reaches the age of 18 years: s9(6).
- A section 8 contact order cannot be made in relation to a child in local authority care: s9(1).

Powers and duties under the order

The court can make an order:

- containing directions as to how it is to be put into effect;
- imposing conditions that must be complied with by any person in whose favour the order is made, who is a parent or has parental responsibility, or with whom the child is living and to whom the conditions are expressed to apply;
- to have effect for a specified period, or containing provisions that are to have effect for a specified period; or
- with 'such incidental, supplemental or consequential provision as the court thinks fit': s11(7).

Application of general principles

- The child's welfare shall be the court's paramount consideration: s1(1).
- Delay is likely to prejudice the welfare of the child: s1(2).
- There is a presumption of no order unless the court considers that to make an order would be better for the child: s1(5).
- The welfare checklist applies (if the application is opposed): s1(4).

Who can apply?

As with a residence order, there are two categories of applicant: those who can apply as of right, and those who require the leave of the court.

As of right
Any parent including:

- the unmarried father;
- a guardian;
- any person who has a residence order in relation to the child: s10(4);
- any party to a marriage, if the child is a child of the family;
- any person with whom the child has been living for at least 3 years;
- a person who has the consent of each person who has a residence order;
- the local authority, if the child is in care; or
- in any other case, each person who has parental responsibility: s10(5).

With leave

- Anyone else, including the child.
- In the case of a local authority foster-parent, then, unless he is a relative of the child, or the child has been living with him for 3 years preceding the application, he must have the consent of the local authority to apply for the court's leave: s9(3).
- For the criteria for granting leave, see section 10(8) and (9).
- In addition, the court is able to make a section 8 order on its own motion; that is, without an application being made: s10(1)(b).

Exclusions

A local authority may not apply for a contact order under this section: s9(2).

Respondents/notice

As provided in the Family Proceedings Rules 1991 and the Family Proceedings Courts (Children Act 1989) Rules 1991.

Venue

Magistrates' court, county court or High Court, although this may be limited by a legal aid certificate.

Duration

A contact order ceases to have effect:

- if the parents live together for a continuous period exceeding 6 months: s11(6);
- when the child reaches the age of 16 years or, in exceptional circumstances, 18 years: s91(10).

Appeal

To the High Court from the magistrates' court, and to the Court of Appeal from the county court or High Court.

Variation and discharge

- Any person entitled to apply for a contact order can apply for its variation or discharge.
- Anyone else shall be entitled to do so if the order was made on his application or if he is named in the contact order: s10(6).
- The order is discharged by a care order: s91(2).

Section 8: Specific Issue Order

Definition

An order giving directions for the purpose of determining a specific question that has arisen, or that may arise, in connection with any aspect of parental responsibility for a child, such as medical treatment, education and religion.

Qualifying criteria

- A section 8 order can be applied for separately or as part of other proceedings.
- Subject to the following restrictions, the court is empowered to make a specific issue order in any family proceedings:
  - no court can make a specific issue order that is to have effect after the child is 16 years old or (in exceptional circumstances) 18 years old: s9(6);
  - a specific issue order cannot be made in relation to a child in local authority care: s9(1);
  - the court cannot make a specific issue order with a view to achieving a result that could be achieved by a residence or contact order, or in any way that is denied to the High Court (by s100(2)): s9(5).

Powers and duties under the order

The court can make an order:

- containing directions as to how it is to be put into effect;
- imposing conditions that must be complied with by any person in whose favour the order is made, who is a parent or has parental responsibility, or with whom the child is living and to whom the conditions are expressed to apply;
- to have effect for a specified period, or containing provisions that are to have effect for a specified period; or
- with such 'incidental, supplemental or consequential provision as the court thinks fit': s11(7).

Application of general principles

- The child's welfare shall be the court's paramount consideration: s1(1).
- Delay is likely to prejudice the welfare of the child: s1(2).
- There is a presumption of no order unless the court considers that to make an order would be better for the child: s1(5).
- The welfare checklist applies (if the application is opposed): s1(4).

Who can apply?

As of right

- Any parent or guardian.
- Any person who has a residence order in relation to the child: s10(4).

With leave

- Anyone else, including the child.
- For the criteria for granting leave, see section 10(8) and (9).
- In addition, the court is able to make a section 8 order on its own motion; that is, without an application being made: s10(1)(b).

Respondents/notice

As provided in the Family Proceedings Rules 1991 and the Family Proceedings Courts (Children Act 1989) Rules 1991.

Venue

Magistrates' court, county court or High Court, although this may be limited by a legal aid certificate.

Duration

Until a further order is made or until the child is 16 years old or (in exceptional circumstances) 18 years old.

Appeal

To the High Court from the magistrates' court, and to the Court of Appeal from the county court or High Court.

Variation and discharge

- Any person entitled to apply for a specific issue order can apply for its variation or discharge.
- Anyone else shall be entitled to do so if the order was made on his application: s10(6).
- The order is discharged by a care order: s91(2).

Section 8: Prohibited Steps Order

Definition

- An order that no step that could be taken by a parent in meeting his parental responsibility for a child, of a kind specified in the order, shall be taken by any person without the consent of the court.
- Orders of this kind might be used to restrain a person with parental responsibility from taking a child out of the country, raising the child in a specified religious denomination, or agreeing to certain specified forms of medical assessment or treatment.

Qualifying criteria

- A section 8 order can be applied for separately or as part of other proceedings.
- The court is empowered to make a prohibited steps order in any family proceedings.
- No court can make a prohibited steps order that is to have effect after the child is 16 years old or (in exceptional circumstances) 18 years old: s9(6).
- A prohibited steps order cannot be made relating to a child in local authority care: s9(1).
- The court cannot make a prohibited steps order with a view to achieving a result that could be achieved by a residence or contact order, or in any way that is denied to the High Court (by s100(2)): s9(5).

Powers and duties under the order

The court can make an order:

- containing directions as to how it is to be put into effect;
- imposing conditions that must be complied with by any person in whose favour the order is made, who is a parent or has parental responsibility, or with whom the child is living and to whom the conditions are expressed to apply;
- to have effect for a specified period, or containing provisions that are to have effect for a specified period; or
- with such 'incidental, supplemental or consequential provision as the court thinks fit': s11(7).

Application of general principles

- The child's welfare shall be the court's paramount consideration: s1(1).
- Delay is likely to prejudice the welfare of the child: s1(2).
- There is a presumption of no order unless the court considers that to make an order would be better for the child: s1(5).
- The welfare checklist applies (if the application is opposed): s1(4).

Who can apply?

There are two categories of applicant:

As of right

- Any parent or guardian.
- Any person who has a residence order in relation to the child: s10(4).

With leave

- Anyone else, including the child. However, the court will not grant a prohibited steps order on the application of a local authority where it considers it should be making an application for a care or supervision order (*Nottinghamshire County Council v. P* [1993] 2 FLR 134).
- For the criteria for granting leave, see section 10(8) and (9).
- The court is able to make a section 8 order on its own motion; that is, without an application being made: s10(1)(b).

Respondents/notice

As provided in the Family Proceedings Rules 1991 and the Family Proceedings Courts (Children Act 1989) Rules 1991.

Venue

Magistrates' court, county court or High Court, although this may be limited by a legal aid certificate.

Duration

Until a further order is made or until the child is 16 years old or (in exceptional circumstances) 18 years old.

Appeal

To the High Court from the magistrates' court, and to the Court of Appeal from the county court or High Court.

Variation and discharge

- Any person entitled to apply for a prohibited steps order can apply for its variation or discharge.
- Anyone else shall be entitled to do so if the order was made on his application: s10(6).
- The order is discharged by a care order: s91(2).

Section 16: Family Assistance Order

Definition

An order providing for a probation or local authority officer to advise, assist and befriend a person named in the order.

Qualifying criteria

The court may only make a family assistance order if:

- it has the power to make an order under Part II (note that it does not have to make a section 8 order); and
- the circumstances of the case are exceptional; and
- it has obtained the consent of every person named in the order other than the child: s16(3).

Powers and duties under the order

- The order requires either a probation officer or an officer of the local authority to be available to advise, assist and (where appropriate) befriend any person named in the order: s16(1).
- The persons who can be named in the order are:
  - any parent or the guardian of the child;
  - any person with whom the child is living or in whose favour a contact order is in force with respect to the child;
  - the child.
- Any person named in the order can be required to take such steps as may be specified to keep the officer informed of the address of any person named and to allow the officer to visit such a person(s).
- Originally, the order was intended to provide for short-term supervision without the requirement of proving the criteria under section 31. It seems to be of limited value as it has had little use.

Application of general principles

- The child's welfare shall be the court's paramount consideration: s1(1).
- Delay is likely to prejudice the welfare of the child: s1(2).
- There is a presumption of no order unless the court considers that to make an order would be better for the child: s1(5).
- The welfare checklist does not apply: s1(4).

Who can apply?

Only the court on its own motion can make the order.

Respondents/notice

Not applicable.

Venue

Magistrates' court, county court or High Court.

Duration

A family assistance order lasts a maximum of 6 months, although a new order can be made at the end of this period.

Appeal

To the High Court from the magistrates' court, and to the Court of Appeal from the county court or High Court.

Variation and discharge

The officer may refer to the court the question of whether a section 8 order should be varied or discharged during the period of a family assistance order: s16(6).

4
Public law orders in the Children Act 1989

Part IV of the Children Act 1989 establishes the conditions that are required to be satisfied before the court can consider making a care or supervision order.

With effect from November 2003, all public law proceedings are subject to procedures set out in the Protocol for Judicial Case Management in Public Law Children Act Cases (Lord Chancellor's Department, 2003). The protocol provides a timetable for proceedings and the duties of those involved in the proceedings.

Children's Guardian

In most public law applications, the court will appoint a Children's Guardian to represent the interests of the child who is the subject of the proceedings. The guardian will be in the employment of the Children and Family Court Advisory and Support Service (CAFCASS).

Threshold criteria

The courts may only make public law orders when satisfied that a child's circumstances meet certain threshold criteria. Establishing these criteria involves assessment of the child, his parents' abilities and his circumstances. The criteria and the assessment required are summarised in Figure 1 and in a series of steps:

Step 1
Is the child suffering, or likely to suffer, harm by way of ill-treatment, impairment of health or impairment of development?

Step 2
If the harm suffered by a child is that of an effect on the child's health or development, then how does this child's health or development compare with that which could be reasonably expected of a similar child?

Step 3
Is this harm significant?

Step 4
Is this harm or its likelihood attributable to the care given to the child or likely to be given to him if the order were not made? Otherwise, is the child beyond parental control?

Step 5
Is the care given to the child not what it would be reasonable to expect a parent to give to him?

Step 6
- Would making an order be better for the child than making no order: s1(5)?
- Consider the welfare checklist: s1(3).
- Remember that the welfare of the child is paramount: s1(1).

The central concept of the criteria is the presence or risk of significant harm. Harm is defined in section 31 as 'ill-treatment or the impairment of health or development'. The Adoption and Children Act 2002, when implemented, extends the definition of harm by the addition of the clause 'including, for example, impairment suffered from seeing or hearing the ill-treatment of another': s120.

Ill-treatment is defined as including sexual abuse and forms of ill-treatment that are not physical, although it must by implication include physical abuse.

Health is defined as physical or mental health, and development as physical, intellectual, emotional, social or behavioural development. Where the question of whether harm suffered by a child is significant turns on the child's health or development, his health or development is to be compared with that which could reasonably be expected of a similar child.

These definitions apply throughout the Children Act and interlink with the definition of a child 'in need' in Part III (see p. 10).

If the case is based on an allegation of actual significant harm, the court has to consider the question of whether a child is suffering significant harm at the time when the local authority acts to protect the child: *Re M (A Minor) (Care Order: Significant Harm)* [1994] 3 All ER 298. If the case is based on a likelihood of significant harm, it is not necessary to prove that harm is more likely to occur than not, but the court does have to be satisfied on a balance of probabilities of the facts on which the likelihood is based: *Re H (Threshold Criteria) (Standard of Proof)* [1996] 1 FLR 80. The court must also be satisfied that the evidence is cogent and commensurate with the seriousness of the allegations.

Fig. 1 Significant harm criteria

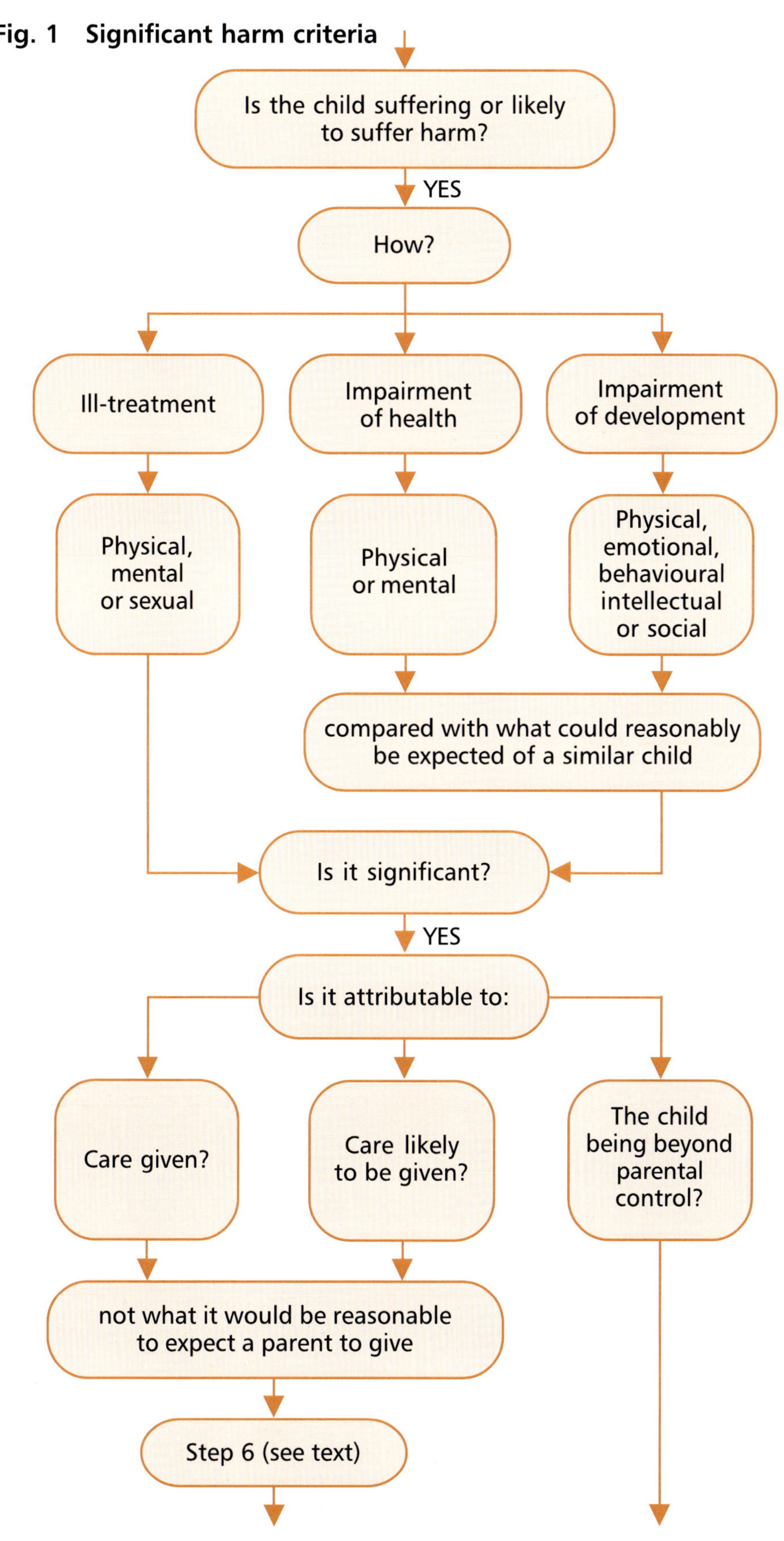

In *Lancashire County Council v. B* [2000] 2 AC 147, the House of Lords considered how the 'attributable' threshold condition (Step 4 in this book) should be applied when the significant harm condition is satisfied but the court is unable to decide which of two or more carers was the perpetrator of the physical harm in question. The House decided that in such 'uncertain perpetrator' cases, the phrase 'the care given to the child' in section 31(2)(b)(i) includes the care given by any of the carers, so that this condition is fulfilled even though the identity of the particular carer who was the perpetrator is not known.

In 'uncertain perpetrator' cases, the correct approach is for the judge conducting the disposal hearing to have regard, to whatever extent is appropriate, to the facts found by the judge at the preliminary hearing. When the facts found at the preliminary hearing leave open the possibility that a parent or other carer was a perpetrator of proved harm, that conclusion cannot be excluded from consideration at the disposal hearing as one of the matters to be taken into account: *Re O and N* (2003) UKHL 18.

Section 1(5)

Even if the threshold criteria are satisfied, there remains a further step for courts to consider (Step 6), that of showing that there are likely to be advantages to the child by making a care or supervision order, which would not accrue if no such order were made. Health care practitioners may find themselves called upon, by virtue of their experience, training and clinical activities, to provide written or oral evidence, or to express expert opinion on these issues.

Other changes to previous legislation

The local authority must provide the court and the parties with its care plan for the child. The care plan should contain its overall aim, the child's needs including those for contact, the views of others (including relevant medical and educational opinion), placement details and a timetable and the arrangements for management and support by the local authority: Care Plans and Care Proceedings under the Children Act 1989 (LAC (99) 29). When implemented, the Adoption and Children Act 2002 will add section 31A to the Children Act 1989 to require the local authority to file and keep under review a care plan for each child.

Care orders are not available for children who fail to attend school (unless they are suffering significant harm) or those facing criminal proceedings before the juvenile courts. The education supervision order is available for those who fail to attend school and, as conditions of supervision orders, the courts may order medical and psychiatric examination and treatment, subject to the consent of the child, where he is deemed capable of understanding.

Section 31: Care Order

Definition

A court order giving parental responsibility for a child to a local authority.

Qualifying criteria

The court may only make a care order if it is satisfied that the child concerned is suffering (or is likely to suffer) significant harm, and that the harm (or likelihood of harm) is attributable to:

- the care given to the child, or likely to be given to him if the order were not made, not being what it would be reasonable to expect a parent to give him; or
- the child being beyond parental control: s31(2).

For elaboration of these criteria see pages 29–32 and Figure 1 on page 31.

Before making a care order, the court must consider the arrangements that the local authority has made, or proposes to make, for affording contact with the child. The court must invite the people involved to the proceedings to comment on these arrangements: s34(11).

Powers and duties under the order

- The local authority is under a duty to receive the child into its care and to keep him in care while the order remains in force: s33(1). This includes providing accommodation for and maintaining the child: s23(1).
- The local authority acquires parental responsibility for the child (s33(3)(a)), which it shares with the parents: s2(7). However, it can determine the extent to which a parent or guardian of the child may meet their parental responsibility in order to safeguard the child's welfare: s33(3)(b) and (4).
- There is a presumption of reasonable contact between child and:
    - a parent;
    - a guardian;
    - a person who held a residence order in respect of the child immediately prior to the making of the care order;
    - any person who had care of the child by virtue of an order of the High Court acting under its inherent jurisdiction before the care order was made: s34(1).
- For specific duties, see sections 23 and 24.
- For specific restrictions on the powers of a local authority under a care order, see section 33(5) to (9).

Application of general principles

- The child's welfare shall be the court's paramount consideration: s1(1).
- Delay is likely to prejudice the welfare of the child: s1(2).
- There is a presumption of no order unless the court considers that to make an order would be better for the child: s1(5).
- The welfare checklist applies: s1(3).
- In practice, these provisions mean that the local authority will be required to file a care plan at court setting out its proposals for the future care of the child.

Who can apply?

A local authority or an 'authorised person' (only *the National Society for the Prevention of Cruelty to Children* (NSPCC) has been so authorised to date): s31(1) and (9). In practice, it is only local authorities that make applications for care or supervision orders.

Venue

To be commenced in the magistrates' court, unless the application arises out of an investigation directed by a higher court or there are relevant existing proceedings in a higher court, but the proceedings may be transferred to the county court or High Court: Children (Allocation of Proceedings) Order 1991.

Respondents/notice

As provided in the Family Proceedings Courts (Children Act 1989) Rules 1991 and the Family Proceedings Rules 1991.

Duration

A care order lasts until the child's 18th birthday unless it is brought to an end earlier: s91(12).

Appeal

To the High Court from the magistrates' court and, with permission, to the Court of Appeal from the county court and the High Court.

Variation and discharge

A care order is discharged by:

- making a residence order: s91(1);
- making a supervision order: schedule 3, paragraph 10;
- the successful application of the child, the local authority or any person with parental responsibility for the child. On such an application, the court can substitute a supervision order for the care order: s39(4).

A care order is terminated by an adoption order or a freeing order: Adoption Act 1976, (ss12 and 18).

Supervision of care plan

If a local authority does not carry out its care plan under the care order, there are the following options for challenge:

- application for discharge of the care order by a parent;
- application for a residence order by a person authorised to do so;
- complaint to the local authority (see pages 11–12 and pages 99–100);
- judicial review if the authority has behaved unreasonably;
- application under section 7 of the Human Rights Act 1998 if the authority has failed to respect the right to family life under Article 8 of the European Convention on Human Rights: *Re M (Care: Challenging Decisions by Local Authority)* [2001] 2 FLR 1300.

On implementation of section 118 of the Adoption and Children Act 2002 and regulations to be made under section 26 of the Children Act 1989, an independent person will be appointed to carry out reviews of children looked after by a local authority; such persons may refer a case to an officer of the Children and Family Court Advisory and Support Service if they consider it appropriate to do so, for example if a care plan has not been carried out.

After-care

A local authority looking after a child has a duty to advise, assist and befriend him with a view to promoting his welfare when they have ceased looking after him: Schedule 2, paragraph 19A (Children Act 1989 as amended by Children (Leaving Care) Act 2000).

Local authorities have a range of duties for 'eligible' and 'relevant' children and 'former relevant' children, who meet the relevant criteria: Schedule 2, paragraph 19B and the Children (Leaving Care) Regulations 2001 (see Chapter 11).

Section 38: Interim Care Order

Definition

A court order giving parental responsibility for a child to a local authority pending a final hearing.

Qualifying criteria

- The court can make an interim care order when adjourning an application for a care or supervision order or giving directions to investigate a child's circumstances under s37(1): s38(1).
- The court may only make an interim care order if it is satisfied that there are reasonable grounds for believing that the circumstances with respect to the child are as mentioned in s31(2): s38(2).

Powers and duties under the order

- The local authority is under a duty to receive the child into its care and to keep him in care while the order remains in force: s33(1). This includes providing accommodation for and maintaining the child: s23(1).
- The local authority acquires parental responsibility for the child (s33(3)(a)), which it shares with the parents: s2(7). However, it can determine the extent to which a parent or guardian of the child may meet their parental responsibility in order to safeguard the child's welfare: s33(3)(b) and (4).
- There is a presumption of reasonable contact between child and:
  - a parent;
  - a guardian;
  - any person who held a residence order in respect of the child immediately prior to the making of the order;
  - any person who had care of the child by virtue of an order of the High Court acting under its inherent jurisdiction before the care order was made: ss34(1) and 31(11).
- For specific duties, see sections 23 and 24.
- For specific restrictions on the powers of a local authority under a care order, see section 33(5) to (9).
- When it makes an interim order, a court has the power to make directions about medical or psychiatric examination or assessment of the child. The mature minor can refuse to submit to such examination: s38(6).

Exclusion orders

The court may make an exclusion requirement in an interim care order requiring a person to leave a dwelling house in which he is living with the child, or a provision prohibiting a person from entering the house, or a provision excluding the person from a defined area in which the house is situated *if* there is reasonable cause to believe that the child will cease to suffer or cease to be likely to suffer significant harm if the person is so excluded *and* another person living in the house is able and willing to give the child the care it would be reasonable to expect a parent to give him and that person consents to the exclusion requirement: s38A. A power of arrest may be attached.

Application of general principles

- The child's welfare shall be the court's paramount consideration: s1(1).
- Delay is likely to prejudice the welfare of the child: s1(2).
- There is a presumption of no order unless the court considers that to make an order would be better for the child: s1(5).
- The welfare checklist applies: s1(3).

Who can apply?

A local authority or an 'authorised person' (the NSPCC): s31(1) and (9).

Venue

To be commenced in the magistrates' court, unless the application arises out of an investigation directed by a higher court or there are relevant existing proceedings in a higher court, but the proceedings may be transferred to the county court or High Court: Children (Allocation of Proceedings) Order 1991.

Respondents/notice

As provided in the Family Proceedings Courts (Children Act 1989) Rules 1991 and the Family Proceedings Rules 1991.

Duration

- Initially an interim care order can be made for 8 weeks with further orders of up to 4 weeks (longer in the case of orders during the first 8 weeks, if the first order was for less than 4 weeks).

- The court, in determining the period for which the order is to be in force, must consider whether any party who was or might have been opposed to the order was in a position to argue his case in full: s38(10).
- There is no limit to the number of orders that can be made (s38(4) and (5)), although the court must have regard to the delay principle (see above) and must establish a timetable for disposal of the proceedings: s32.
- Normally an interim care order will be made as a holding order pending a final hearing at which the parties can present their long-term plans for the child. If the court is not satisfied that the local authority has presented a coherent care plan, it may make a further interim care order: *Re S (Minors) (Care Order: Implementation of Care Plan); Re W (Minors) (Care Order: Adequacy of Care Plan)* [2002] UKHL 10, [2002] 2 WLR 720, [2002] 1 FLR 815.

Appeal

To the High Court from the magistrates' court and, with permission, to the Court of Appeal from the county court and the High Court.

Variation and discharge

- An interim care order may be discharged on the application of any person with parental responsibility, the child or the local authority (s39(1)) or on making a residence order: s91(1).
- Application to discharge a direction may be made by the parties to the proceedings and any person named in the direction.

Section 34: Contact with Children in Care

Definition

An order requiring a local authority to permit a specified person to have contact with a child in its care.

Qualifying criteria

- The child must be in care.
- There is a presumption that the child in care will be allowed reasonable contact with those entitled to apply for contact: s34(1).
- Before making a care order, the court must consider the arrangements that the local authority has made or proposes to make for affording any person contact with the child and invite the parties to comment on those arrangements: s34(11).
- The court can make an order even though no application for such an order has been made: s34(5).

Powers and duties under the order

The court can impose such conditions as it considers appropriate: s34(7).

Application of general principles

- The child's welfare shall be the court's paramount consideration: s1(1).
- Delay is likely to prejudice the welfare of the child: s1(2).
- There is a presumption of no order unless the court considers that to make an order would be better for the child: s1(5).
- The welfare checklist applies: s1(3).

Who can apply?

The following have a right to apply for an order allowing contact:

- the child or the local authority;
- the child's parent or guardian;
- the person in whose favour a residence order existed immediately prior to the making of the care order;
- any person who, immediately before the making of the care order, had care of the child by virtue of an order of the High Court acting under its inherent jurisdiction.

Anyone else can apply for contact with the leave of the court.

Venue

To be commenced in the magistrates' court, unless there are relevant proceedings in a higher court, but the proceedings may be transferred to the county court or High Court.

Respondents/notice

As provided in the Family Proceedings Courts (Children Act 1989) Rules 1991 and the Family Proceedings Rules 1991.

Duration

The order lasts until the child reaches the age of 18 years or the date specified in the order, unless discharged.

Appeal

From the magistrates' court to the High Court and, with permission, to the Court of Appeal from the county court or High Court.

Variation and discharge

- The child, local authority or person named in the order may apply for variation or discharge: s34(9).
- An order may be varied without a court order in accordance with the provisions set out in the Contact with Children Regulations 1991.

Refusal of contact

The local authority and the child can apply for an order authorising contact to be refused: s34(4).

Contact with children in care is ultimately a matter for the court. If the judge concludes that the benefits of contact outweigh the disadvantages of disrupting the local authority's long-term plans, which are inconsistent with contact, he must refuse the local authority's application to terminate contact: *Re E (A Minor) (Care Order: Contact)* [1994] 1 FLR 146.

Section 31: Supervision Order

Definition

A court order requiring a local authority or probation officer to advise, assist and befriend a child.

Qualifying criteria

The court may only make a supervision order if it is satisfied:

- that the child concerned is suffering (or is likely to suffer) significant harm, and
- that the harm (or likelihood of harm) is attributable to:
  - the care given to the child, or likely to be given to him if the order were not made, not being what it would be reasonable to expect a parent to give him; or
  - the child being beyond parental control: s31(2).
- For elaboration of these criteria see pages 29–32 and Figure 1 on page 31.

Powers and duties under the order

- The supervisor is under a duty to:
  - advise, assist and befriend the supervised child;
  - take such steps as are reasonably necessary to give effect to the order; and
  - where the order is not wholly complied with, or the supervisor considers that the order may no longer be necessary, to consider whether or not to apply to the court for its variation or discharge: s35(1).
- The supervision order may require the child to comply with specified directions given by the supervisor and that the responsible person shall take all reasonable steps to ensure that the child complies with those directions: Schedule 3, part 1.
- The court can include a requirement concerning the examination or treatment of a child, but it must be satisfied that, where the child has sufficient understanding to make an informed decision, he consents to this and that satisfactory arrangements have been made for the examination or treatment: Schedule 3, paragraph 5(5).

Application of general principles

- The child's welfare shall be the court's paramount consideration: s1(1).
- Delay is likely to prejudice the welfare of the child: s1(2).
- There is a presumption of no order unless the court considers that to make an order would be better for the child: s1(5).
- The welfare checklist applies: s1(3).

Who can apply?

A local authority or an 'authorised person': s31(1) and (9).

Venue

To be commenced in the magistrates' court, unless the application arises out of an investigation directed by a higher court or there are relevant existing proceedings in a higher court, but the proceedings may be transferred to the county court or High Court: Children (Allocation of Proceedings) Order 1991.

Respondents/notice

As provided in the Family Proceedings Court (Children Act 1989) Rules 1991 and the Family Proceedings Rules 1991.

Duration

A supervision order lasts for 1 year with a possible extension of up to 3 years: Schedule 3, paragraph 6(1) and (4).

Appeal

From the magistrates' court to the High Court and, with permission, to the Court of Appeal from the county court or High Court.

Variation and discharge

A supervision order may be discharged by:

- making a care order: s91(3);
- successful application by the child, any person with parental responsibility, or the supervisor: s39(2).

Section 36: Education Supervision Order

Definition

A court order requiring a local education authority to supervise a child to ensure that the child is properly educated.

Qualifying criteria

The court must be satisfied that the child is of compulsory school age and is not being properly educated: s36(3). A child is properly educated only if he is receiving efficient, full-time education suitable to his age, ability and aptitude or any special educational needs he may have: s36(4).

An education supervision order cannot be made in respect of a child in local authority care: s36(6).

Powers and duties under the order

- The supervisor is under a duty to advise, assist and befriend, and give directions to the supervised child and his parents in such a way as will, in the opinion of the supervisor, secure the child's proper education: Schedule 3, paragraph 12.
- The child, and the parent (if asked), may be required to keep the supervisor informed of any change in address and to allow the supervisor to visit the child wherever he is living: Schedule 3, paragraph 16.
- If directions are not complied with, the supervisor must consider what further steps to take in exercise of his powers under the Act: schedule 3, paragraph 12.
- If the child persistently fails to comply with any direction given under the order, the local education authority must notify the local authority, which must investigate the circumstances of the child: Schedule 3, paragraph 19.
- A parent who persistently fails to comply with a direction given under an education supervision order is guilty of an offence: Schedule 3, paragraph 18.

Application of general principles

- The child's welfare shall be the court's paramount consideration: s1(1).
- Delay is likely to prejudice the welfare of the child: s1(2).
- There is a presumption of no order unless the court considers that to make an order would be better for the child: s1(5).
- The welfare checklist applies: s1(3).

Who can apply?

A local education authority: s36.

Venue

Proceedings start in the magistrates' court but may be transferred to the county court or High Court.

Respondents/notice

- As provided in the Family Proceedings Courts (Children Act 1989) Rules 1991 and the Family Proceedings Rules 1991.
- The local education authority must consult the appropriate social services committee before making an application: s36(8).

Duration

- An education supervision order lasts for 1 year.
- Extension may be made for up to 3 years and there can be more than one extension: Schedule 3, paragraph 15.
- The order automatically ceases on:
  - making a care order;
  - the child reaching school-leaving age.

Appeal

To the High Court from the magistrates' court and, with permission, to the Court of Appeal from the county court and the High Court.

Discharge

The child, parent or local education authority can apply for discharge: Schedule 3, paragraph 17.

Section 38: Interim Supervision Order

Definition

A court order requiring a local authority or probation officer to advise, assist or befriend a child pending a final hearing.

Qualifying criteria

- The court can make an interim supervision order when:
  - adjourning an application for a care or a supervision order;
  - giving directions to investigate a child's circumstances under sections 37(1) and 38(1).
- The court shall make an interim supervision order when it makes a residence order in care proceedings, unless the child's welfare will be satisfactorily safeguarded without one: s38(3). However, the court may only make the order if it is satisfied that there are reasonable grounds for believing that the circumstances with respect to the child are as mentioned in s31(2): s38(2).

Powers and duties under the order

- When it makes an interim supervision order, the court has the power to make directions about medical or psychiatric examination or assessment of the child. The mature minor can refuse to submit to such examination: s38(6).
- Directions under Schedule 3 may also be imposed (see Supervision Order), but not those under paragraphs 4 and 5.

Application of general principles

- The child's welfare shall be the court's paramount consideration: s1(1).
- Delay is likely to prejudice the welfare of the child: s1(2).
- There is a presumption of no order unless the court considers that to make an order would be better for the child: s1(5).
- The welfare checklist applies: s1(3).

Who can apply?

A local authority or an 'authorised person': s3(1) and (9).

Venue

To be commenced in the magistrates' court, unless the application arises out of an investigation directed by a higher court or there are relevant existing proceedings in a higher court, but the proceedings may be transferred to the county court or High Court.

Respondents/notice

As provided in the Family Proceedings Courts (Children Act 1989) Rules 1991 and the Family Proceedings Rules 1991.

Duration

- An interim supervision order can initially be made for 8 weeks with further orders of up to 4 weeks (longer in the case of orders during the first 8 weeks, if the first order was for less than 4 weeks).
- The court, in determining the period for which the order is to be in force, must consider whether any party who was or might have been opposed to the order was in a position to argue his case in full: s38(10).
- There is no limit to the number of orders that can be made (s38(4) and (5)), although the court must have regard to the delay principle (see above) and must establish a timetable for disposal of the proceedings: s32.

Appeal

To the High Court from the magistrates' court and, with permission, to the Court of Appeal from the county court and the High Court.

Variation and discharge

- An interim supervision order may be varied or discharged on the application of any person with parental responsibility, the child or the supervisor: s39(2).
- A person who is not entitled to apply for the order to be discharged, but with whom the child is living, can apply for the variation of the order in so far as it imposes a requirement that affects that person: s39(3).

5 Orders in the Children Act 1989 for protecting children

Part V of the Children Act, which concerns the protection of children, introduced the child assessment order, and replaced the place of safety order with the emergency protection order. The place of safety order was an *ex parte* order (on, or in the interests of, one side only); the emergency protection order can be *ex parte*, but the Act awards parents the right to be heard by a court shortly after a successful application for an emergency protection order. The police have separate powers to protect children.

Practitioners should be aware of published research on child protection processes: see *Child Protection: Messages from Research* (Department of Health, 1995*b*).

The duty to investigate

Section 47 imposes on the local authority duties to investigate. Where a local authority is informed that a child who lives or is found in its area is the subject of an emergency protection order or is in police protection, or the authority has reasonable cause to suspect that a child who lives or is found in its area is suffering or likely to suffer significant harm, the authority is required to make sufficient enquiries to enable it to decide whether it should take any action to safeguard or promote the welfare of the child. This includes considering:

- provision of services under Part III;
- proceedings under section 31;
- proceedings under Part V, as set out below.

Section 43: Child Assessment Order

Definition

A court order providing for an assessment of a child who is suspected to be suffering, or likely to suffer, significant harm. This order has been little used in practice.

Qualifying criteria

The court may make a child assessment order if it is satisfied that:

- the applicant has reasonable cause to suspect that the child is suffering, or is likely to suffer, significant harm; and
- an assessment of the state of the child's health or development, or the way in which he has been treated is required to enable the applicant to determine whether or not the child is suffering or is likely to suffer significant harm; and
- it is unlikely that such an assessment will be made or be satisfactory in the absence of an order: s43(1)(a) to (c).

The court may also consider whether the more appropriate order in the circumstances is an emergency protection order and, if so, make one, if the criteria are satisfied: s43(3).

Powers and duties under the order

- The child assessment order requires any person who is in a position to produce the child to:
  - produce the child to such person as may be named in the order;
  - comply with such directions relating to the assessment of the child as the court thinks fit to specify in the order: s43(6).
- The child can only be kept away from home in accordance with directions and for a period or periods specified in the order, if it is necessary for the purposes of the assessment: s43(9).
- The order authorises any person carrying out the assessment to do so in accordance with the terms of the order, but the mature minor can refuse to submit to such assessment: s43(7) and (8).

Application of general principles

- The child's welfare shall be the court's paramount consideration: s1(1).
- Delay is likely to prejudice the welfare of the child: s1(2).
- There is a presumption of no order unless the court considers that to make an order would be better for the child: s1(5).
- The welfare checklist does not apply: s1(4).

Who can apply?

A local authority or an 'authorised person': s43(1).

Venue

To be commenced in the magistrates' court, unless the application arises out of an investigation directed by a higher court or there are relevant existing proceedings in a higher court, but the proceedings may be transferred to the county court or High Court: Children (Allocation of Proceedings) Order 1991.

Respondents/notice

The applicant shall take such steps as are reasonably practicable to ensure that notice is given to:

- the child's parents;
- any person with parental responsibility for the child who is not a parent;
- any other person caring for the child;
- any person in whose favour a contact order is in force or who is allowed contact with the child under section 34;
- the child: s43(11).

Duration

- The child assessment order lasts for a maximum of 7 days from a date specified in the order: s43(5).
- There can be no further application for a child assessment order within 6 months without the leave of the court: s91(15).

Appeal

To the High Court from the magistrates' court, and to the Court of Appeal from the county court and the High Court.

Variation and discharge

The applicant and any person referred to in section 43(11) (see above) may apply for variation or discharge: Family Proceedings Rules 1991, r4.2(2) and Family Proceedings Courts (Children Act 1989) Rules 1991, r2.

Sections 44 and 45: Emergency Protection Order

Definition

A court order authorising the detention of a child in safe accommodation.

Qualifying criteria

The court may make an emergency protection order if, but only if, it is satisfied that:

- where the applicant is 'any person', there is reasonable cause to believe that the child is likely to suffer significant harm if he is not removed to accommodation provided by, or on behalf of, the applicant, or if he does not remain in the place in which he is being accommodated: s44(1)(a);
- where the applicant is a local authority, inquiries are being made with respect to the child under section 47(1)(b) which are being frustrated because access is unreasonably refused and the applicant has reasonable cause to believe access is required urgently: s44(1)(b);
- where the applicant is an 'authorised person', the applicant has reasonable cause to suspect that a child is suffering, or is likely to suffer, significant harm, and the applicant is making inquiries which are being frustrated because access is unreasonably refused and the applicant has reasonable cause to believe access is required urgently: s44(1)(c).

Powers and duties under the order

An emergency protection order requires any person who is in a position to produce the child to do so if required: s44(4)(a). It authorises:

- removal of the child to accommodation provided by the applicant, where necessary, in order to safeguard the welfare of the child: s44(4)(b) and (5)(a);
- prevention of the removal of the child from a hospital or other place in which he was being accommodated immediately before the making of the order: s44(4)(b)(ii);
- the applicant to have parental responsibility for the child: s44(4)(c).

While the order is in force, the court has the power to give directions with respect to:

- the contact that is or is not to be allowed between the child and any named person;
- medical or psychiatric examination or other assessment of the child (s44(6)), although the mature minor can refuse to submit to such examination: s44(7).

The court may issue a warrant authorising any constable to assist (using force if necessary) any person attempting to exercise powers under an emergency protection order who has been prevented (or is likely to be prevented) from doing so by being refused entry to premises and/or access to the child: s48(9).

Exclusion orders

The court may make an exclusion requirement in the emergency protection order requiring a person to leave a dwelling house in which he is living with the child, or a provision prohibiting a person from entering the house, or a provision excluding the person from a defined area in which the house is situated *if* there is reasonable cause to believe that the child will cease to be likely to suffer significant harm if the person is so excluded *and* another person living in the house is able and willing to give the child the care it would be reasonable to expect a parent to give him and that person consents to the exclusion requirement: s44A. A power of arrest may be attached.

Application of general principles

- The child's welfare shall be the court's paramount consideration: s1(1).
- Delay is likely to prejudice the welfare of the child: s1(2).
- There is a presumption of no order unless the court considers that to make an order would be better for the child: s1(5).
- The welfare checklist does not apply: s1(4).

Who can apply?

'Any person', a local authority or an 'authorised person': s44(1).

Venue

- Application is normally made to a single magistrate or to a sitting magistrates' court.
- The county court or High Court, where that court has directed an investigation or is hearing relevant proceedings, has power to make the order.

Respondents/notice

- With the consent of the justices' clerk, the application may be made without notice to a single magistrate.
- The Family Proceedings Court (Children Act 1989) Rules 1991 give detailed requirements with regard to notice (if it is possible in the circumstances) and provision of information after the order has been made.

Duration

- An emergency protection order lasts a maximum of 8 days, with the possibility of an extension for a maximum of a further 7 days if the court 'has reasonable cause to believe that the child concerned is likely to suffer significant harm if the order is not extended': s45(4) to (6).
- Irrespective of these limits, the child must be returned as soon as it is safe to do so: s44(10).
- Where the 8-day period ends on Christmas Day, Good Friday, a bank holiday, or a Sunday, the court may specify a period ending at noon on the first later day: s45(2).

Appeal

There is no appeal against any matter relating to an emergency protection order: s45(10) (as amended by the Courts and Legal Services Act 1990 Schedule 14) and *Essex County Council v. F* [1993] 1 FLR 847.

Discharge

Application to discharge may be made on 1 day's notice by:

- the child;
- a parent, or other person having parental responsibility;
- any person with whom the child was living immediately before the order was made: s45(8).

No application to discharge may be heard within the first 72 hours of the order (s45(9)), nor can there be an application for the discharge of an extended emergency protection order: s45(11).

A person cannot apply for discharge if he was given notice of the original hearing and was present at the hearing: s45(11).

Variation

Application may be made for variation of a direction (s44(9)) by: the parties; the children's guardian; the local authority in whose area the child is ordinarily resident; and any person named in the direction: Family Proceedings Rules 1991, r4.2(4) and Family Proceedings Courts (Children Act 1989) Rules 1991, r2.

Section 46: Police protection

Power

- A constable has power under section 46 to take a child into police protection.
- He must have reasonable cause to believe that the child would otherwise be likely to suffer significant harm.
- He may remove the child to suitable accommodation or take steps to prevent his removal.

Duration

- The child may not be kept in police protection for more than 72 hours.
- If it is necessary to extend the period, application must be made for an emergency protection order.

Section 50: Recovery Order

Definition

A court order directing the production of a child or the disclosure of his or her whereabouts.

Qualifying criteria

The court may make a recovery order where it has reason to believe that the child:

- has been unlawfully taken or kept away from the responsible person named in an emergency protection order or care order, or from police protection;
- has run away or is staying away from the responsible person;
- is missing: s50(1).

Powers and duties under the order

The recovery order:

- operates as a direction to anybody in a position to do so to produce the child on request to any authorised person;
- authorises the removal of the child by any authorised person;
- requires any person who has information about the whereabouts of the child to disclose that information if asked to do so by a constable or officer of the court;
- authorises a constable to enter premises specified in the order and search for the child, using reasonable force if necessary: s50(3).

Application of general principles

- The child's welfare shall be the court's paramount consideration: s1(1).
- Delay is likely to prejudice the welfare of the child: s1(2).
- There is a presumption of no order unless the court considers that to make an order would be better for the child: s1(5).
- The welfare checklist does not apply: s1(4).

Who can apply

A person with parental responsibility by virtue of an emergency protection order or a care order; or, where the child is in police protection, the designated officer: s50(4).

Venue

Proceedings are commenced in the magistrates' court unless the application arises out of a court-directed investigation, but the proceedings may be transferred to the county court or High Court.

Respondents/notice

As provided in the Family Proceedings Courts (Children Act 1989) Rules 1991 and the Family Proceedings Rules 1991.

Duration

Until enforcement.

Appeal

To the High Court from the magistrates' court, and to the Court of Appeal from the county court and the High Court.

6
Consent to assessment, examination and treatment

In general, legally valid consent is required from a person of whatever age before medical assessment and treatment can be given. There is a legal presumption that, in relation to medical issues, all adults have the capacity to make their own medical decisions. In the case of children or young people, however, this presumption does not apply.

Assessment and treatment (and this includes touching without consent) can constitute an assault. For consent to be valid:

- the person who is the patient must be capable of consenting;
- the consent must be freely given;
- the patient consenting must be given suitable information.

The exceptions to this general proposition include:

- giving treatment in emergency circumstances where the patient lacks capacity, for example where the patient is unconscious (and did not make a valid advance refusal of treatment before losing consciousness); and
- where statute allows for treatment to be given without consent (e.g. under powers given in Part IV of the Mental Health Act 1983).

Defining capacity

In a number of cases, the courts have developed tests to be used in assessing capacity. These tests are essentially aids to analysing medical evidence. For example, in the case of MB, the court had to decide whether a pregnant woman had capacity to refuse consent to a caesarean section: *Re MB (Medical Treatment)* [1997] 2 FLR 426. The evidence before the court was that her needle phobia made her incapable of making a decision. The court applied the following principles in assessing her capacity. It presumed the patient to have the capacity to make a treatment decision unless she was unable:

- to comprehend and retain the information that is material to the decision, especially as to the likely consequences of having or not having the treatment in question; or
- to believe the information; or
- to use the information and weigh it in the balance as part of the process of arriving at the decision.

The courts have not provided any specific guidance in relation to considering the capacity of children or young people. The guidance in *Re C [1994] 1 FLR 31* and *Re MB [1997] 2 FLR 426* involving adults should be the starting point and the guidance can then be developed and refined.

In particular, guidance issued by the British Medical Association in Chapter 4 of *Consent, Rights and Choices in Health Care for Children and Young People* (British Medication Association, 2001) should be followed. Some pointers taken from that association's guidelines are listed here.

- Competence is dependent on the task in hand. It should be constantly reassessed as children develop and as different treatments, tasks or challenges are faced.
- Children of the same age differ significantly in their ability and willingness to participate. It is important not to approach young patients with preconceptions about ability.
- Consent, like treatment, is a process and not a single event, and doctors often have an ongoing relationship with a patient that permits sound judgements about competence over time.
- Ability to participate can be enhanced by allowing time for discussions and ensuring that appropriate information is provided.
- Unless there are time constraints because of the nature of the illness, adequate time should be set aside for an exploration of the question of competence.
- Information from parents or carers who know and love the child or young person is of great importance, although doctors should be wary of relying solely on what could be an overly subjective view. Other people, such as teachers, play specialists, nursing staff and social workers may be in a good position to provide an objective appraisal.
- A general practitioner who has known the patient for a long time may be well placed to evaluate competence and provide important information to other professionals on this point. It must, however, be borne in mind that children constantly change, and reliance should not necessarily be placed on an assessment that is not contemporaneous.

If an adult is regarded as lacking capacity, then medical treatment can be provided on the following basis: 'a doctor can lawfully operate on or give other treatment to adult patients who are incapable of consenting to his doing so, provided that the operation or treatment is in the best interests of such patients. The operation or treatment will be in their best interests only if it is carried out in order either to save their lives or to ensure improvement or prevent deterioration in their physical or mental health': *Re F* [1989] 2 All ER 545.

Treatment decisions

In its report on the review of the Mental Health Act 1983, the Expert Committee wrote: 'The law relating to the treatment of children suffering from mental disorder is in need of clarification. The current multiplicity of legal provisions creates a climate of uncertainty, professionals are unsure of their authority and of the legal and ethical entitlements of the children in their care' (Department of Health 1999*b:* Para. 13.1). This section is therefore intended to summarise, in as logical a fashion as possible, the current law in this area. A flow diagram (Figure 2) is also included at the end as a reminder to readers; and the authors are very grateful to Julian Beezhold for this contribution.

Finally, readers are reminded that, as this book goes to print, it is likely that the government's proposals to change mental health law will result in significant changes to the rights of minors to consent to, or refuse, medical treatment for mental disorder.

Parental responsibility

The Children Act 1989 introduced the concept of parental responsibility, emphasising that the duty to care for one's child and to raise him or her to moral, physical and emotional health is the fundamental task of parenthood. Prior to the Act, case law had established that the older the child, the less extensive parental responsibility may become. Lord Denning observed in *Hewer v. Bryant* [1969] 3 All ER 578: 'the legal right of a parent ends at the 18th birthday, and even up till then, it is a dwindling right which the courts will hesitate to enforce against the wishes of the child, the older he is. It starts with a right of control and ends with little more than advice.'

The House of Lords in *Gillick v. West Norfolk and Wisbech Area Health Authority* [1986] AC 112 emphasised that the parental power to control a child exists not for the benefit of the parent but for the benefit of the child. Lord Scarman said: 'Parental rights clearly do exist, and they do not wholly disappear until the age of majority ... But the common law has never treated such rights as sovereign or beyond review and control. Nor has our law ever treated the child as other than a person with capacities and rights recognised by law. The principle of the law ... is that parental rights are derived from parental duty and exist only so long as they are needed for the protection of the person and property of the child ... parental rights yield to the child's right to make his own decisions when he reaches a sufficient understanding and intelligence to be capable of making up his own mind on the matter requiring decision.'

The person with parental responsibility will usually be one of the parents. Mothers have parental responsibility automatically when the child is born; fathers also obtain parental responsibility automatically if they were married to the mother at the time of the birth of the child, or if they marry the mother after the birth of the child. Fathers also obtain parental responsibility if they make a 'parental responsibility agreement' with the mother, or obtain a parental responsibility order from the courts. Non-parents may also obtain parental responsibility; for example, a local authority obtains parental responsibility if a care order is granted in its favour.

Where more than one person has parental responsibility, it is not necessary to seek consent from them all. Valid consent may be obtained from any person with parental responsibility. Application to the court may be necessary to proceed to provide treatment if consultation with the parent is thought not to be in the interests of the child (for example, if abuse by the parent is alleged). This may mean that service providers might initiate such an application, or participate in applications brought by social services departments. In circumstances in which parents refuse consent for treatment of their child that is thought by a doctor to be necessary, the use of court proceedings must also be considered.

A child's consent to medical treatment

Although, in an emergency, a doctor may undertake treatment if the well-being of a child could suffer by delay, it is normal practice to obtain the consent of a parent as an exercise of their parental responsibility. There may be circumstances, however, in which children will decide for themselves.

The position of young people aged 16 or 17 years
Section 8(1) of the Family Law Reform Act 1969 provides that a child of 16 years or over may consent 'to any surgical, medical or dental treatment which, in the absence of consent, would constitute a trespass to his person, [and the consent] shall be as effective as it would be if he were of full age; and where a minor has by virtue of this section given an effective consent to any treatment it shall not be necessary to obtain any consent for it from his parent or guardian.'

The position of children and young people under 16 years old
In certain circumstances, a child of less than 16 years of age, but who is of sufficient age and understanding can give valid consent. In *Gillick v. West Norfolk and Wisbech Area Health Authority* [1986] AC 112, it was held that a doctor may lawfully prescribe contraception for a girl less than 16 years of age without the consent of her parents. She could have legal capacity to give a valid consent to contraceptive advice and treatment, including medical examination. Whether she gave a valid consent in any particular case would depend on the circumstances, including her intellectual capacity to understand advice. There is no absolute parental right requiring the parent's consent to be sought.

Speaking of medical treatment generally, Lord Scarman said:

> 'It will be a question of fact whether a child seeking advice has sufficient understanding of what is involved to give a consent valid in law. Until the child achieves the capacity to consent, the parental right to make the decision continues save only in exceptional circumstances. Emergency, parental neglect, abandonment of the child, or inability to find the parents are examples of exceptional situations justifying the doctor proceeding to treat the child without parental knowledge and consent, but there will arise, no doubt, other exceptional situations in which it will be reasonable for the doctor to proceed without the parent's consent.'

Applying this to contraceptive advice and treatment, he said: 'There is much that has to be understood by a girl under the age of 16 if she is to have legal capacity to consent to such treatment. It is not enough that she should understand the nature of the advice which is being given: she must also have a sufficient maturity to understand what is involved.'

In the same case, Lord Fraser established five preconditions that would justify a doctor in prescribing contraceptive treatment:

- that the girl (although under 16 years of age) will understand his advice;
- that he cannot persuade her to inform her parents or to allow him to inform the parents that she is seeking contraceptive advice;
- that she is very likely to begin or to continue having sexual intercourse with or without contraceptive treatment;
- that unless she receives contraceptive advice or treatment her physical or mental health or both are likely to suffer; and
- that her best interests require him to give her contraceptive advice, treatment or both without the parental consent.

Refusal of consent

Although the Gillick decision might have been taken to imply that a 'Gillick-competent' child could also veto any proposed treatment, Lord Donaldson MR subsequently said in *Re R (A Minor) (Wardship: Medical Treatment)* [1992] Fam 11, CA that this is not so. According to his judgment, all that was decided in the Gillick case was that a competent child could give a valid consent, not that such a child could withhold consent.

This approach was followed in *Re W (A Minor) (Medical Treatment)* [1993] Fam 64, CA, in which it was further held that section 8 of the Family Law Reform Act 1969 does not empower young people aged 16 or 17 years to veto medical treatment. In most cases the consent of somebody with parental responsibility, be it a parent or local authority, will be sufficient, and application to the court should not be necessary: *Re K, W and H (Minors) (Consent to Treatment)* [1993] 1 FLR 854.

Powers of local authorities

Where a care order is in force, the local authority has parental responsibility and may give consent. The parent retains responsibility and, as a matter of good practice, should still be consulted. If the child is accommodated, the local authority does not automatically have parental responsibility, although the parent may have delegated responsibility to the authority on the child's entry to accommodation.

In the absence of any responsibility, the local authority could seek a court direction under section 8 of the Children Act or through the exercise of the inherent jurisdiction of the High Court.

Powers of the courts

A decision by a parent to consent or refuse to consent to an operation may be overridden by the court: *Re C (A Minor) (Medical Treatment)* [1993] Fam 64, [1992] 4 All ER 627, CA. It is more likely that the court would find that a child refusing essential treatment would not be Gillick-competent.

Where a child has made an informed decision to refuse treatment, but his condition has become life-threatening or seriously injurious, certain statutory provisions, for example where the child is subject to a supervision order, would appear to give the child the right to override a court order for treatment. However, the court may make an appropriate order. In *Re J (A Minor) (Medical Treatment)* [1992] 2 FLR 165, the Court of Appeal held that treatment of a minor for anorexia could be authorised against her wishes, although the decision about treatment was one for the doctor.

In *Re C (A Minor) (Wardship: Medical Treatment)* [1990] Fam 26, CA, it was held that, where a ward of court was terminally ill, the court would authorise treatment to relieve the child's suffering.

Consent to medical or psychiatric examination or assessment

The Children Act 1989 provides that the court may direct that a child undergo a medical or psychiatric examination or other assessment if one of four orders are in force:

- an emergency protection order, under section 44;
- a child assessment order, under section 43;
- an interim care order, under section 38(6);
- a supervision order, under section 35.

The provisions also state that, notwithstanding the court direction, the child who is of sufficient understanding to make an informed decision can refuse to submit to the examination or assessment.

Nonetheless, it has been held that the High Court, in the exercise of its inherent jurisdiction, can override the child's refusal to consent under section 38(6): *South Glamorgan County Council v. W and B* [1993] 1 FLR 574.

Summary

Figure 2 (pages 64–65) summarises the issues involved in gaining legally valid consent relating to medical and other interventions for minors.

Consent to a service for people who misuse substances

Questions on providing drugs, or material in conjunction with the use of drugs, such as needles or syringes, could come within the Gillick principles. Careful thought should be given in each case as to how the provision and operation of, for example, a needle and syringe exchange can be justified as a medical treatment.

The Gillick decision requires that any action should be based on a proper assessment of the circumstances of the case. It refers to assessment by a doctor and clinical judgement, but when dealing with the mental health of children, a competent assessment may be made by others. A practitioner must be able to show the competence to analyse and carry out a reasoned application of the Gillick criteria. It is particularly important to maintain the records as evidence of the assessment process used and advice given.

The five preconditions that emerge from the Gillick case (adapted from Lord Fraser's judgment: see page 61), could be adapted and applied to providing a service related to problems of substance use and misuse. Such preconditions might be:

- that the young person (although under 16 years of age) understands the advice;
- that the young person cannot be persuaded to inform his or her parents or to allow them to be informed that the young person is seeking advice or treatment relating to substance use or misuse;
- that the young person is very likely to begin or to continue using substances with or without the advice or treatment;
- that unless the young person receives advice on or treatment for the use of substances, his or her physical or mental health (or both) are likely to suffer; and
- that the young person's best interests require the practitioner to give advice and/or treatment without parental consent.

Legally valid consent would be ineffective if the provision of advice or treatment relating to use or misuse of substances were in itself a criminal offence. Therefore, it is important for any practitioner to ensure that the actions involved in the treatment are not themselves capable of interpretation as a criminal offence, for example as drug-pushing. If the practitioner is to avoid possible prosecution for being an accessory to the unlawful use of drugs, there must be an honest intention to act in the best interests of the young person.

Figure 6.2 ***Cont'd***

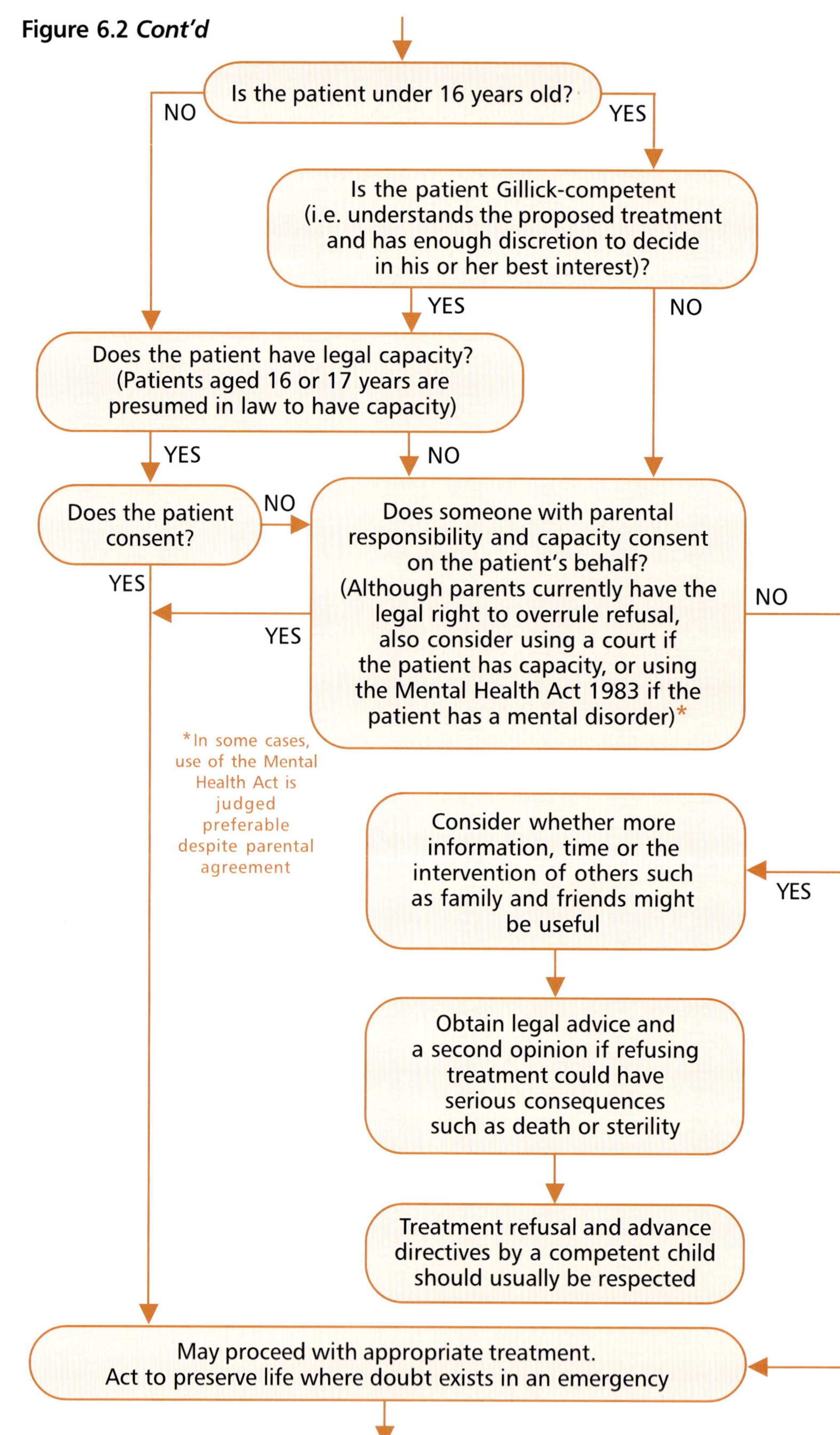

Figure 6.2 Treatment consent and refusal for children. The editor is grateful to Julian Beezehold for permission to redraw his original figure.

Capacity testing

- Does the patient understand the nature, benefits and risks of the proposed treatment?
- Does the patient understand the alternatives to treatment and the consequences of not having treatment?
- Can the patient retain and believe this information long enough to weigh it in the balance and make a choice?
- Can the patient make the choice voluntarily (free from pressure)?

See pp. 57–66 for more information on capacity and consent

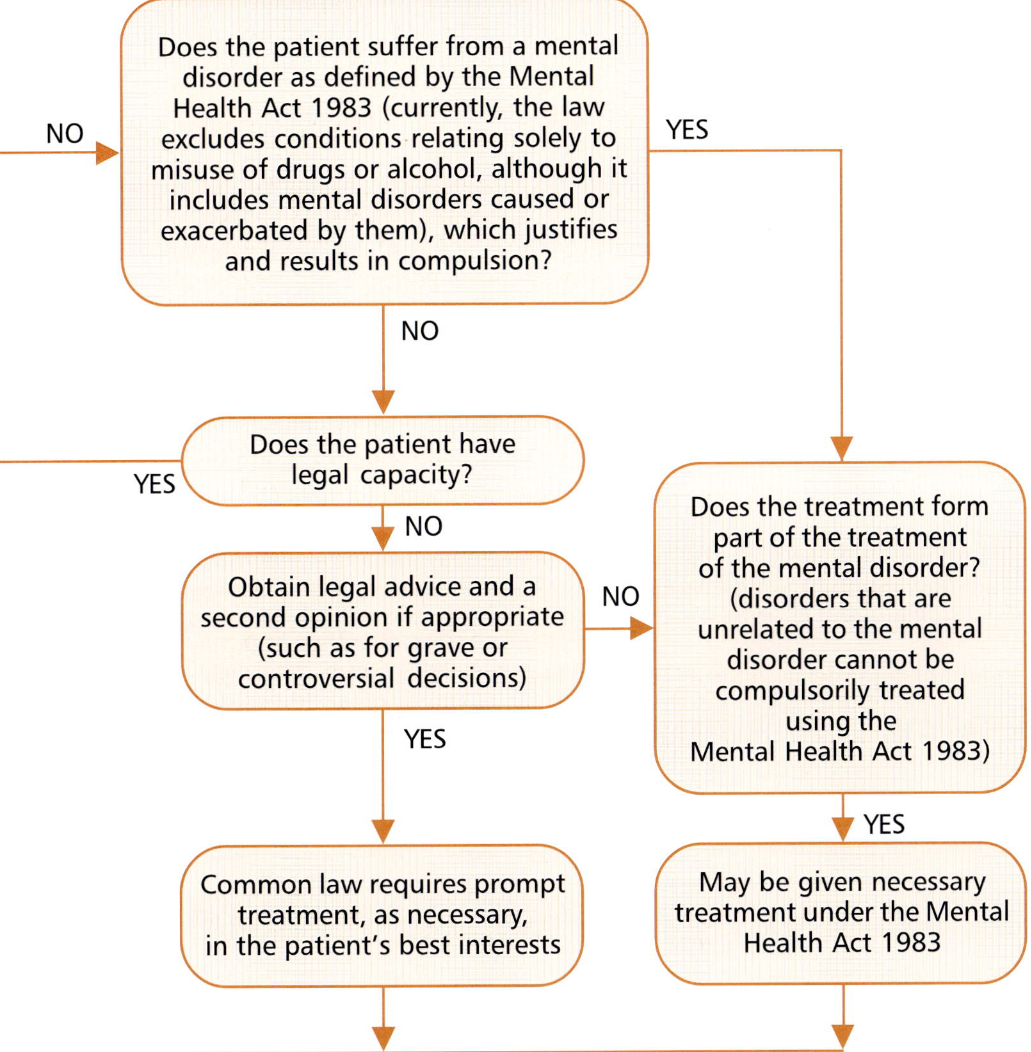

Consent for children and young people in police detention

In England and Wales, the Codes of Practice of the Police and Criminal Evidence Act 1984 require that persons in police detention are considered juveniles if they are, or appear to be, under the age of 17 years.

In such circumstances, the custody officer must inform an 'appropriate adult' and ask that adult to come to the police station to see the detained person. In the case of a juvenile, an appropriate adult is often the young person's parent or guardian. However, where no other suitable candidate is available, it can be any responsible adult aged 18 years or over who is not a police officer or employed by the police. Thus, there may be occasions when the person acting as an appropriate adult may not have parental responsibility.

In all but exceptional circumstances, a juvenile must not be interviewed or asked to provide or sign a written statement in the absence of an appropriate adult. For any procedure that requires the consent of a juvenile, the consent of the parent or guardian is also required (unless the child is under 14 years old, in which case the consent of the parent or guardian is sufficient in its own right).

When a medical examination is required for forensic purposes, legally valid consent should be obtained after a full explanation of the extent and purpose of the examination from the juvenile in the presence of the appropriate adult. Consideration should be given to obtaining the consent of the person with parental responsibility.

7
Admission of minors to hospital

Although the principles set down below all apply to all forms of medical treatment, the focus in this chapter is on providing treatment for mental disorder. Children and young people are sometimes admitted as in-patients to paediatric wards for treatment of mental disorder. This may be arranged informally, or under section, if the criteria for using the Mental Health Act are met.

Children and young people aged less than 16 years

Where a child or young person under the age of 16 is regarded as 'Gillick competent' by the admitting doctor/s and has the capacity to make a decision for himself or herself, the child or young person can make his or her own decision as to admission and treatment as an in-patient in hospital, irrespective of the wishes if his or her parent or guardian.

If the child or young person lacks capacity, then somebody with parental responsibility may arrange for his or her admission. If it is considered by an interested party, such as a local authority, that such an admission would not be in the child's interests, then recourse could be had to the courts.

Young people aged 16–17 years

A 16- or 17-year-old who is capable of expressing his or her own wishes can, as in the case of 'Gillick competent' children discussed above, make his or her own decision as to admission and treatment in hospital. Where a 16- or 17-year-old is incapable of expressing his or her own wishes, the consent of a person with parental responsibility should be obtained.

Refusal of admission

Even if a child or young person does not want to be admitted to hospital, it would be lawful with the consent of somebody with parental responsibility to arrange for that child's admission. Given that the child's or young person's liberty may have to be restricted and their right to liberty may be violated, then, when medical treatment for mental disorder is being considered, use of the Mental Health Act to authorise admission must always be considered. In other cases, section 25 of the Children Act may be applicable, or a section 8 order may be sought.

Informal admission for treatment of mental disorder

The Mental Health Act 1983 (s131) provides that 'a minor who has attained the age of 16 years and is capable of expressing his own wishes' can enter hospital for treatment of mental disorder on an informal basis. If the child has been detained, and the detention ends, then the child can remain in hospital on an informal basis.

Admission under compulsion

Chapters 8 and 9 review the statutory basis for restricting the liberty of children and young people who are under 18 years old: Chapter 8 reviews the powers given by the Children Act 1989, in particular section 25 and its implications; and Chapter 9 summarises the provisions of the Mental Health Act 1983. Readers are referred to those chapters for more detail about the circumstances in which young people can be lawfully admitted to hospitals or other facilities for children when compulsion is required. Chapter 10 reviews matters that should be taken into consideration when deciding which legislative framework to use.

Some implications of legislation for hospital in-patient treatment

Two provisions in the Children Act 1989 have important consequences for in-patient and day patient mental health units.

Strategic health authorities, local health boards, primary care trusts and NHS trusts that intend to provide, or do provide, accommodation for a child for a consecutive period of 3 months or more are required to notify the responsible social services department: ss 85 and 86. In Wales, the Carlile Review recommended in 2002 that this period be reduced voluntarily by the Director of NHS Wales to 1 month regardless of breaks and weekend leave (National Assembly for Wales, 2002).

The Children (Secure Accommodation) Regulations 1991 extend the application of section 25 of the Children Act, which relates to restricting children's liberty, to children accommodated by the NHS and who are not detained under the provisions of the Mental Health Act 1983. Even if children are placed in a health service secure unit by their parents, without any local authority involvement, then the provisions of section 25 apply.

The Code of Practice to the Mental Health Act 1983 has been amended as a result of these Regulations.

The Mental Health Act (s116) contains an important provision in relation to children. Where a child or young person is in care and admitted to hospital (not only psychiatric hospitals), then the local authority is obliged to arrange visits and 'to take other steps in relation to the patient ... as would be expected'.

8

Restricting liberty under the Children Act 1989

The liberty of children may only be restricted in accordance with provisions set out in section 25 of the Children Act 1989, the Children (Secure Accommodation) Regulations 1991, and the Children (Secure Accommodation) (No. 2) Regulations 1991. The Children Act 1989 Guidance and Regulations, vol. 4, *Residential Care* (Department of Health, 1991*a*), referred to subsequently as the Guidance, Volume 4, supplements the statutory provisions. Secure tracking units are not considered here, since at the time of writing, the provisions relating to them had not come into force.

Secure accommodation is defined as 'accommodation provided for the purpose of restricting liberty': Children Act 1989, s25(1). The Guidance recognises that the interpretation of this term is ultimately a matter for the court, but states: 'it is important to recognise that any practice or measure which prevents a child from leaving a room or building of his own free will may be deemed by the court to constitute restriction of liberty. For example, while it is clear that locking a child in a room, or part of a building, to prevent him leaving voluntarily is caught by the statutory definition, other practices which place restrictions on freedom of mobility (for example, creating a human barrier), are not so clear cut' (Guidance, Volume 4, paragraph 8.10).

Use of secure accommodation by local authorities for children looked after by them, and for children accommodated by health authorities, local health boards, primary care trusts and NHS trusts and local education authorities, and children accommodated in children's homes, nursing homes and mental nursing homes, is permitted only where the criteria in section 25 of the 1989 Act are fulfilled.

Local authorities have a duty under the Children Act 1989 to take reasonable steps to avoid placing children within their area in secure accommodation (Schedule 2, paragraph 7). The guidance states: 'Restricting the liberty of children is a serious step which must be taken only when there is no appropriate alternative. It must be a 'last resort' in the sense that all else must first have been comprehensively considered and rejected – never because no other placement was available at the relevant time, because of inadequacies in staffing, because the child is simply being a nuisance or runs away from his accommodation and is not likely to suffer significant harm in doing so, and never as a form of punishment ... Secure placements, once made, should be only for so long as is necessary and unavoidable. Care should be taken to ensure that children are not retained in security simply to complete a predetermined assessment or 'treatment' programme' (Guidance, Volume 4, paragraph 8.5).

Section 25 provides that secure accommodation may not be used in respect of a child unless it appears that:

(a) (i) he has a history of absconding and is likely to abscond from another type of accommodation; and

(ii) if he absconds, he is likely to suffer significant harm;

or

(b) if he is kept in any other type of accommodation he is likely to injure himself or other persons: s25(1).

A child may only be kept in secure accommodation for as long as the relevant criteria apply. Furthermore, a child under the age of 13 years shall not be placed in secure accommodation in any children's home without the prior approval of the Secretary of State. Such approval shall be subject to such terms and conditions as the Secretary of State sees fit (reg 4 of the Children (Secure Accommodation) Regulations 1991).

The maximum period during which a child's liberty may be restricted without the authority of a court is 72 hours, either consecutively or in aggregate in any period of 28 days (reg 10(1) of the Children (Secure Accommodation) Regulations 1991). There is some relaxation of this restriction to meet difficulties caused by the period expiring on a Saturday, a Sunday or public holiday (reg 10(3) of the Children (Secure Accommodation) Regulations 1991).

The Children Act definition of a child as 'any person under the age of 18 years' defines the upper age limit on young people coming into secure accommodation with the exception of certain accommodated children (see below).

Children to whom section 25 does not apply

The restrictions on the use of secure accommodation do not apply to:

- children detained under any provision of the Mental Health Act 1983 (as they are provided by the mental health legislation);
- children detained under section 53 of the Children and Young Persons Act 1933, concerning the punishment of certain grave crimes.

Children accommodated under the following provisions may not have their liberty restricted in any circumstances:

- young people over 16 years old who are being accommodated under section 20(5) of the Children Act;
- children in respect of whom a child assessment order under section 43 of the Children Act has been made and who are kept away from home pursuant to that order.

Applications to court

Applications to court for authority to use secure accommodation may only be made by or on behalf of a local authority looking after a child or, as extended by No. 2 regulation, where the child is accommodated by a health authority, local health board, primary care trust or NHS trust, by that health agency.

Application is made to the family proceedings court, except where the matter arises in the context of a case already before a county court or High Court (in which case application is made to that court), or to the youth court, when criminal proceedings are involved.

The criteria applicable to use of secure accommodation by local authorities are modified in the case of children looked after by them who are:

- children detained using powers given by the Police and Criminal Evidence Act 1984, section 38(6);
- children remanded to local authority accommodation under the Children and Young Persons Act 1969, section 23, but only if:
  - the child is charged with, or has been convicted of a violent or sexual offence, or of an offence punishable, in the case of an adult, with imprisonment for a term of 14 years or more; or
  - the child has a recent history of absconding while remanded to local authority accommodation, and is charged with, or has been convicted of an imprisonable offence alleged or found to have been committed while he was so remanded.

In the latter circumstances, secure accommodation may not be used unless it appears that any accommodation other than that provided for the purpose of restricting liberty is inappropriate because:

- the child is likely to abscond from such other accommodation; or
- the child is likely to injure himself or other people if he is kept in other accommodation.

Evidence

When considering whether to make an order, the court is under a duty to consider whether the relevant criteria for keeping a child in secure accommodation under section 25 are satisfied.

The extent to which the welfare principles under section 1 of the Children Act 1989 have to be taken into account has been a matter of difference of opinion. The Department of Health guidance states that:

> 'It is the role of the court to safeguard the child's welfare from inappropriate or unnecessary use of secure accommodation, both by satisfying itself that those making the application have demonstrated that the statutory criteria in section 25(1) or regulation 6 as appropriate have been met and by having regard to the provisions and principles of s1 of the Act. The court must therefore be satisfied that the order will positively contribute to the child's welfare and must not make an order unless it considers that doing so would be better for the child than making no order at all' (Guidance, Volume 4, paragraph 5.7).

The Court of Appeal has held that the welfare of the child is relevant but not the paramount consideration and that the principles of section 1 do not apply: *Re M (a Minor) (Secure Accommodation Order)* [1995] 1 FLR 418, CA. The role of the court is to decide whether the evidence shows that the agency making an application should be given the power to take such a serious step.

A secure accommodation order gives power to a local authority to detain a child in secure accommodation, but it does not compel detention; in other words, the order is permissive, as it does not require the child to be kept in secure accommodation. An order, therefore, should be for no longer than is necessary and unavoidable, and may have a short-term usefulness to break a pattern of absconding: *W v. North Yorkshire County Council* [1993] 1 FCR 693.

Initially, the maximum period of an authorisation is 3 months. The court should not automatically make an order for 3 months but must consider what is necessary for the circumstances of the case: *Re W (A Minor) (Secure Accommodation Order)* [1993] 1 FLR 692. Authorisation may be renewed for further periods of up to 6 months at a time (regs 11 and 12 of the Children (Secure Accommodation) Regulations 1991).

Where an application for a secure accommodation order is made in family proceedings, hearsay evidence is admissible. It is desirable to have a psychiatric report available as evidence: *R(J) v. Oxfordshire County Council* [1992] 3 All ER 660. The court must give reasons for its decision: Family Proceedings Courts (Children Act 1989) Rules 1991, rule 21.

Control and restraint of children and young people

Questions about treatment of children and young people include those with respect to control and restraint, seclusion, de-stimulation and 'time out'. There is little statutory or common law regulating these methods of treatment, and it is necessary to look to general principles.

Certainly, practitioners should be aware that any method of intervention involving restraint or restriction of liberty could be subject to the provisions in section 25 of the Children Act 1989. In respect of any method of treatment, the question of informed and legally valid consent arises.

A situation that causes particular concern about lawful consent is where a young person who is being provided with in-patient psychiatric care on the basis of consent given by someone with parental responsibility (see pages 59–61 and 67–68) also requires seclusion or restraint for a lengthy period. Although the intervention may be sanctioned by the parent, if the effect is to restrict the young person's liberty beyond the 72 hour period allowed by the Children Act 1989 (see pages 69–71 and this page relating to discharge), then section 25 may apply.

The Children's Homes Regulations 2002 cover the conduct of homes and securing the welfare of children living there. The regulations provide for controlling and disciplining children in homes. Physical control or restraint of a child must of its nature be at least a technical assault. The authority for the assault must arise through the proper restriction of liberty, self-defence or consent. Reference should also be made to *Guidance on Permissible Forms of Control in Residential Care* (Department of Health, 1993).

Discharging children and young people from secure accommodation

When a child is accommodated by a local authority, health authority, local health board, primary care trust or NHS trust, plans should be made to discharge the child when the authorisation to continue to detain the child expires.

There may be occasions when a child cannot immediately be accommodated at home or elsewhere. Although plans should be made sufficiently well in advance to ensure that suitable accommodation is available, it does not seem to us to be unlawful to permit the child to continue to live on the same premises. We think that a precondition that should be applied in circumstances of this kind is ensuring that both the child and the adults holding parental responsibility are advised that the child can leave the premises if the child or the responsible parents so wish. If such a condition were met, our opinion is that the circumstances would no longer come within the provision of being 'kept' within accommodation provided for the purpose of restricting liberty.

It is appropriate to restate a general principle here: if a child is accommodated in secure provision (as described in this chapter), any person who has parental responsibility may remove the child from such accommodation at any time.

9
Restricting liberty under the Mental Health Act 1983

In certain circumstances, the Mental Health Act 1983 provides an alternative statutory basis for restricting the liberty of a child or young person by way of admission to hospital, and then conducting an assessment and providing certain forms and types of treatment under compulsion. In general terms, there is no age limit on use of the Mental Health Act 1983. The Act provides four main routes of admission to psychiatric hospitals or units:

- informal admission (s131);
- civil admission (compulsory admission following professional recommendations and decision – Part II of the Act);
- admission from court to hospital (Part III of the Act);
- transfer from prison to hospital (Part III of the Act).

This chapter deals with civil admissions and the consequences of detention and compulsion.

Definition of mental disorder

A person can be compulsorily detained in hospital for assessment or treatment on the grounds that he or she suffers from a mental disorder. Mental disorder is broadly defined under the Act as 'mental illness, arrested or incomplete development of mind, psychopathic disorder and any other disorder or disability of the mind': s1(2).

Mental illness is not defined in the Act. Mental impairment, severe mental impairment and psychopathic disorder are defined as follows:

- severe mental impairment – 'a state of arrested or incomplete development of mind that includes severe impairment of intelligence and social functioning and is associated with abnormally aggressive or seriously irresponsible conduct on the part of the person concerned';

- mental impairment – 'a state of arrested or incomplete development of mind (not amounting to severe mental impairment) that includes significant impairment of intelligence and social functioning and is associated with abnormally aggressive or seriously irresponsible conduct on the part of the person concerned';
- psychopathic disorder – 'a persistent disorder or disability of mind (whether or not including significant impairment of intelligence) that results in abnormally aggressive or seriously irresponsible conduct on the part of the person concerned'.

A person cannot be treated as being mentally disordered for any purposes of the Act on the grounds of promiscuity, immorality, sexual deviance or misuse of alcohol or drugs.

The courts have adopted a restrictive approach to the concept of serious irresponsibility. In one case, a 17-year-old individual with a learning disability wanted to return home from the care of a local authority. The local authority regarded her as being at some risk if she did so. As the court regarded the urge to return home as 'almost universal', it concluded that F's determination could not be regarded as seriously irresponsible: *Re F (Mental Health Act: Guardianship)* [2000] 1 FLR 192.

Civil admission (Part II of the Act)

Criteria

The civil admission process, commonly referred to as 'sectioning', is usually carried out by a specialist social worker known as an Approved Social Worker (ASW) who makes the application on the basis of two medical recommendations. The most common orders sought are:

Admission for assessment or assessment followed by treatment: section 2

Section 2 provides that a person may be detained using powers given by the Act for a period of up to 28 days on the grounds that the person:

- is suffering from a mental disorder of a nature or degree that warrants detention in hospital for assessment or assessment followed by medical treatment for at least a limited period;
- ought to be detained in the interests of his own health and safety or with a view to the protection of others.

Admission for treatment: section 3

Section 3 provides that a person may be detained using powers given by the Act for an initial period of up to 6 months (which can be renewed) on the grounds that the person:

- is suffering from mental illness, severe mental impairment, psychopathic disorder or mental impairment and the mental disorder is

of a nature or degree that makes it appropriate for the person to receive medical treatment in hospital; and
- it is necessary for the health or safety of the person or for the protection of others that he should receive such treatment and it cannot be provided unless the person is detained under Section 3.

Where the person is considered to suffer from psychopathic disorder or mental impairment, a further condition must be met before an application for treatment under section 3 may be made: this is that such treatment is likely to alleviate or prevent deterioration in the person's condition. This is known as the 'treatability' test.

The meaning of 'nature' and 'degree'

The word 'nature' refers to the particular mental disorder, its chronicity, its prognosis and the propensity of the patient to relapse; 'degree' refers to the current manifestation of the illness: *R v. MHRT for the South Thames Region ex parte Smith* [1999] COD 148.

Nearest relative

Establishing who is the nearest relative

The nearest relative is the person who, owing to his or her relationship to the patient, has been given certain powers and rights in connection with the patient's admission to, and detention in, hospital. Section 26 of the Mental Health Act 1983 sets out the list of people who may be the patient's nearest relative. It is necessary to consider this list in the light of the patient's individual circumstances to ascertain who is the nearest relative. If a patient has two relatives of equal standing (for example, father and mother), the elder of the two is the nearest relative.

Where a patient is a child (that is, any person under the age of 18 years) who is in the care of a local authority, the local authority is deemed to be the child's nearest relative except where the child is married: s27.

Although the child's nearest relative will usually be a person with parental responsibility, it cannot always be assumed that this is the case. The Code of Practice underlines the importance of always identifying who has parental responsibility (Code of Practice, paragraph 31.5).

Consultation with the nearest relative

The Approved Social Worker must, before making an application under section 2 or within a reasonable time after it, take steps to inform the nearest relative of the patient's detention and of the nearest relative's power to discharge the patient: s11(3). The ASW must consult with the nearest relative before making an application under section 3 unless such consultation is not reasonably practicable or would involve unreasonable delay. In the case of section 3, if the nearest relative objects to the application under section 3 being made, it cannot go ahead unless the county court displaces the nearest relative: ss11(4), 29.

Patients cannot choose their own nearest relatives. This may impose certain problems for ASWs, who might, for example, be required to consult a nearest relative who has abused, or allegedly abused, a patient, or from whom a patient is estranged.

By 2000, the Government had accepted that the failure of the existing Mental Health Act to allow a patient to nominate another person as a nearest relative, where the patient reasonably objects to a particular person acting in that capacity, breaches the patient's human rights. The Government, therefore, agreed to amend the Mental Health Act (*JT v. United Kingdom* [2000] 1 FLR 909). This amendment has not yet been introduced and the courts have recently declared that in this area the Mental Health Act 1983 is incompatible with Article 8 of the European Convention of Human Rights (*R (M) v. Secretary of State*, CO/4744/2002).

Patients already in hospital

An application for compulsory detention under section 2 or 3 may be made in respect of a patient who is already in hospital on an informal basis. This also applies to minors. The Act also allows patients to be detained in hospital for short periods to allow time for the admission procedure to be completed.

Care and treatment of detained patients in hospital

Consent to treatment

The Mental Health Act 1983 provides for circumstances in which medical treatment for mental disorder may be given when the patient either refuses to give or is incapable of giving consent. The provisions for such compulsory treatment are set out in Part IV of the Act. The provisions apply to most detained patients, in particular patients detained under sections 2 and 3. The Act sets out requirements and safeguards before certain treatments for mental disorder – notably electroconvulsive therapy (ECT) – can be administered without a detained patient's consent.

Medication for the mental disorder can be given without consent or a second opinion being sought but only for the first 3 months of a patient's detention. Subsequently, the safeguards centre on the opinions of a Second Opinion Approved Doctor (SOAD), who is appointed by the Mental Health Act Commission, which runs the service, and whose authorisation is required for administration of psychotropic medication after patients have been detained for 3 months, whether or not they consent. In the case of ECT, treatment at any time, if the patient does not consent, must be authorised by a SOAD. Section 62 allows both medication and ECT to be given without these particular safeguards in urgent cases.

Particular arrangements are included in the law for patients recommended to receive psychiatric treatments that are considered irreversible. In short, irreversible psychiatric treatments cannot be carried out on any patient (whether informally admitted or compulsorily detained) without authorisation given by a panel appointed by the Mental Health Act Commission.

Certain treatments may be given without either the consent of the patient or the involvement of the SOAD provided the treatment is for the patient's mental disorder:

> 'The consent of a patient shall not be required for any medical treatment given to him for the mental disorder from which he is suffering, not being treatment falling within section 57 or 58 above, if the treatment is given by or under the direction of the Responsible Medical Officer' (s63).

No special procedures need be followed before the treatment can be imposed. Medical treatment is defined in section 145 as including 'nursing, and also includes care, habilitation and rehabilitation under medical supervision'.

Section 63 provides for medical treatment for mental disorder without the patient's consent. Treatments for physical conditions may only be given under section 63 if such treatment is sufficiently connected to the treatment for the patient's mental disorder. Various court decisions have held that certain treatments may be given under section 63:

- feeding by nasogastric tube of a person diagnosed as suffering from anorexia nervosa: *Riverside Health NHS Trust v. Fox* [1994] 1 FLR 614; see also the Mental Health Act Commission guidance Note 3 on anorexia nervosa (issued August 1992 and updated March 1999);
- treatment ancillary to the treatment for the patient's mental disorder (treating the symptom or the consequence of the mental disorder): *B v. Croydon District Health Authority* [1995] 1 All ER 683.

There are definite limits to treatment under section 63. For example, the court has ruled that a man with schizophrenia was entitled to refuse treatment for gangrene on the basis that the treatment for the gangrene 'was entirely unconnected with the mental disorder': *Re C (Adult: Refusal of Medical Treatment)* [1994] 1 All ER 819. A second example is that of caesarean section: a court has ruled that a caesarean section could be undertaken under section 63, but only if it was a necessary part of the overall treatment of the patient's mental disorder: *Tameside and Glossop Acute Services Trust v. CH* [1996] 1 FLR 762.

Responsible medical officer

The term 'Responsible Medical Officer' (RMO) is defined in section 34(1) as the 'medical practitioner in charge of the treatment of the patient'. This definition applies to doctors who acquire particular responsibilities for patients who are detained using the powers of the Mental Health Act. We recognise that the term is frequently used colloquially on a much wider basis; however, we strongly advise against inappropriate use in this way in order to avoid confusion and misunderstanding.

Leave of absence

The RMO may grant leave to a detained patient (s17), subject to any conditions that the RMO considers necessary in the interests of the patient or to protect other persons. Only the RMO may grant leave and the power may not be delegated.

Discharge from hospital

When the period of detention of the section under which the patient is detained expires, the patient is free to leave the hospital. In addition, the following people have the power to discharge a patient detained under the Act before the specified period is over:

- the RMO;
- the nearest relative ;
- a Mental Health Review Tribunal (MHRT);
- the hospital managers.

Section 145(1) of the Mental Health Act 1983, and subsequent statutory instruments and regulations that have recognised the changes in the structures of the NHS in England and the NHS in Wales subsequent to 1983, define who are the managers in NHS hospitals. The definition covers the statutory body or bodies responsible for the hospital. Most of the managers' responsibilities may be delegated to employees or officers, apart from the power to discharge patients which can only be exercised by members of a committee formed for that specific purpose.

10
Choosing between alternative legal frameworks

Choosing the most appropriate legal framework for enforcing the care of young people with serious mental disorders is a cause of concern for many professionals. Sometimes the path is clear, but the choice is not always easy. There may be a variety of reasons for this. One appears to be lack of familiarity in using the Mental Health Act with children. The authors are not alone in this impression: 'One problem faced by services is the relative infrequency of admission of children and adolescents under the Act' (*Ninth Biennial Report 1999–2001*: Mental Health Act Commission (2001), paragraph 6.42). Few ASWs have professional currency in their training to work with children, and the frequency of child and adolescent psychiatrists conducting assessments under the requirements of the Mental Health Act is low.

The majority of children who require in-patient treatment for mental disorder are treated as informal patients on the authority of a person with parental responsibility. Where statutory compulsion is used, the vast majority of young people are detained using powers given in the Mental Health Act. Secure accommodation orders are only occasionally used, typically for young people with learning disabilities who are exhibiting challenging behaviours.

The authors believe that part of the challenge can be tackled by assisting professionals to think through the clinical situations they face in a structured way, in which they return to the core principles that lie behind each of the legislative frameworks. Therefore, this chapter offers pointers that readers might find helpful when deciding which route to take when both the Children Act 1989 and the Mental Health Act 1983 are available. In reality, the choice is most often between a statutory route, usually invoking the Mental Health Act, and informal admission with the agreement of a person with parental responsibility.

In identifying pointers, a range of considerations has to be taken into account. The Children Act may appear less stigmatising as it does not specifically refer to mental disorder, and its use may be seen as reflecting social and family failure rather than a problem located in the mental health of an individual young person. However, the Children Act 1989, unlike Part IV of the Mental Health Act 1983, does not provide specific powers to enforce medical treatment, or to safeguard the rights of detained patients. The safeguards provided by the Mental Health Act include the review of detention by Mental Health Act managers and Mental Health Review Tribunals, and the general oversight of the Mental Health Act Commission. Treatment on the basis of parental consent offers an apparently less stigmatising option but may not best protect the rights of the patient, particularly if compliance is an issue. On the other hand, the Mental Health Act 1983 is not specifically oriented towards children and adolescents, and their needs and circumstances. Some have argued that its underlying principles and safeguards are insufficient to protect the interests of children and young persons in every circumstance in which it would be possible to apply the Act.

In addition, it would be unrealistic for us not to recognise that being detained under the Mental Health Act 1983 might be perceived as being more stigmatising. Although it is difficult to identify any formal stigmatising consequences that flow from having been detained under the Act, there is clearly a risk of informal consequences, often based on prejudice. In considering these possibilities (for example, having difficulty in gaining employment), it is important to clarify whether the risk is a consequence of having received in-patient mental health care or of having been detained under the Act and, not infrequently, it is the former.

When evaluating the legal framework within which an individual child should be treated, the breadth of the concept of treatment needs to be understood. Treatment for children and young people may encompass both detention in a secure environment and the imposition of what the lay person would more easily recognise as medical treatments, such as those referred to in Part IV of the Mental Health Act 1983.

Unlike the Mental Health Act 1983, the Children Act 1989 does not specifically provide for a child's decision about medical treatment to be overridden. Consent will usually depend on an adult exercising parental responsibility (see Chapter 6). If there is a dispute, the court can make a section 8 order specifying the steps to be taken (see pages 15 and 22–23). Where the Children Act does provide that the child who has sufficient understanding to make an informed decision may refuse to undergo a medical or psychiatric examination or assessment, the High Court can make an order overriding the refusal (see page 62). Where the court has made a secure accommodation order under section 25 of the Children Act, the order authorises non-consensual detention in a therapeutic environment, but decisions about treatment must still be dealt with by way of applying common law principles.

Underlying principles

Set out below is a set of guiding principles and some pointers that may be helpful for professionals to take into account when considering the appropriate legal framework, especially when it is proposed to treat a child or younger person without their consent. We hope that these suggestions will not only help to ensure that many of the major considerations will be addressed by those responsible for identifying the appropriate legal framework, but that they will also contribute to professional reflective learning and to a continuing national debate about the principles and the considerations that should underlie such decisions.

In our opinion, when considering the appropriate legal framework, the provider of treatment must, in each case:

- have sufficient understanding of the relevant legal provisions;
- have easy access to competent legal advice;
- keep in mind the importance of ensuring that the child's care and treatment is managed with clarity, consistency and within a recognisable framework; and
- attempt to select the least stigmatising and restrictive option that is consistent with the care and treatment objectives for that patient.

Pointers

The following pointers are derived from the authors' pooled experience.

Human rights

Which legal framework best protects the human rights of both child and parents (see Chapter 1, pages 1–4)?

Discrimination and stigma

It is important that any professional judgement is carefully thought through and based upon a realistic assessment of the relevant considerations. The possibility of discrimination and stigma should be taken into account. However, professionals and managers should endeavour to be clear about the potential sources and impacts of matters of this kind. For example, could any stigma envisaged be related more to the nature of the care and treatment required than the legislative framework chosen, or vice versa?

Parental involvement

Involving those who have parental responsibility is a factor that should always be considered. A child can be treated with the consent of any person having parental responsibility without the necessity for statutory intervention. If a child is detained using powers given by the Mental Health Act 1983, the parent will usually be the nearest relative and must be consulted about admission. Professionals should consider whether this is desirable, particularly when abuse by a parent is alleged. Consulting the nearest relative may not be desirable or therapeutically indicated when there is an allegation of abuse.

Specific treatment decisions

Decisions to treat children or young people should always be discussed with them and with the person having parental responsibility for them, if available. Refusal of a child or young person to be medically treated can be overridden by the consent of an individual with parental responsibility. If both of them refuse, and treatment is in the child's best interests, a court order may be sought under section 8 (see pages 15–18 and 22–26) or by use of the inherent jurisdiction of the High Court. Such an approach may have the benefit of allowing the specific proposed treatment to be addressed and the wishes of the child to be represented.

Due process

Detention under the Mental Health Act 1983 provides an objective legal framework involving third-party statutory agencies, which protects the rights of patients more effectively than overriding a patient's choice by way of the admission and treatment of the child or young person on the authority of someone with parental responsibility. In the latter circumstance, there is an absence of procedural and legal safeguards.

Safeguards

It is important to remember that the provisions of Part IV of the Mental Health Act 1983 afford safeguards when a child or young person's refusal of treatment for mental disorder is overridden by compulsion. These safeguards apply to providing certain forms of treatment, particularly administration of medication for mental disorder after 3 months and ECT. They apply to detained persons whether or not they consent to certain components of the treatment proposed.

Age specificity

The Mental Health Act 1983 is not age-specific. It does not infantilise and so may allow the treatment provided to be focused on the nature of the illness itself.

Assessing the objectives of the treatment

The specific purpose of the intervention in the child's life should be clarified and evaluated. For instance, is the objective of the compulsory detention assessment or treatment? Relevant considerations include the length of time that the child requires treatment and detention, and the severity or longevity of the illness. For example, some seriously ill adolescents might require treatment using powers given by the Mental Health Act 1983, whereas seriously self-harming offenders with a psychiatric component to their problem might require detention under the Children Act 1989. The balance in evaluating these options lies between the need for containment and the need for medical treatment of the mental disorder.

Review and audit

Involving the child in any legal process is another important factor to be considered. Under the Children Act 1989, a children's guardian may be appointed by the court, and the reasons for and benefits of the course proposed in the application itself will be argued before the court. The child may also be represented separately by a solicitor.

Some people have expressed concern about detention under the Mental Health Act 1983, in relation to external review. Although admission under the provisions of this Act can only take place according to specific legal criteria, there is no external audit of the admission process. However, the continuing need for detention is externally reviewed by the Mental Health Review Tribunals, and the provisions of the Act with regard to consent to treatment apply. Both secure accommodation orders under the Children Act 1989 and the powers of compulsion afforded by the Mental Health Act 1983 are time-limited, with established renewal, review and complaints procedures.

11
Placements, after-care and other services

Section 23 of the Children Act 1989 requires local authorities to provide children with accommodation while they are in their care and to maintain them. Where a child is subject to an interim care order or a care order these provisions should work in conjunction with the care plan (see pages 33–40).

Before a local authority begins to look after a child, or as soon as practicable afterwards, it shall make immediate and long-term arrangements for placing the child and for promoting the welfare of the child to be placed: the Arrangements for Placement of Children (General) Regulations 1991.

These provisions should ensure that a proper admissions policy is in place for every establishment and a plan made for every child. The plan should contain:

- the criteria for admission;
- the objectives of the placement;
- the way of achieving those objectives;
- the outcome expectations; and
- the sequel to the placement, which should provide a context for after-care.

However, in the authors' experience, the extent to which these provisions are actually implemented is questionable.

Children in need

On page 10, we noted that 'a child is in need if he is unlikely to achieve or maintain, or to have the opportunity of achieving or maintaining, a reasonable standard of health or development without the provision of services by a local authority under Part III'. Part III of the Children Act 1989 gives powers and duties to local authorities to provide services for children and their families. There is a general duty placed on local authorities to safeguard and promote the welfare of children in their area who are in need and, so far as is consistent with that duty, to promote the upbringing of such children by their families by providing a range and level of services appropriate to those children's needs: s17(1).

Part III of the Children Act 1989 also requires local authorities to produce children's services plans setting out their provision of services. Strategic health authorities, local health boards, primary care trusts and NHS trusts should be consulted in this process.

When assessing the needs of children and families, local authorities will have regard to guidance in the *Framework for the Assessment of Children in Need and their Families* (Department of Health, 2000*a*; National Assembly for Wales, 2001*b*) and *Assessing Children in Need and their Families: Practice Guidance* (Department of Health, 2000*b*).

Leaving care

The Children (Leaving Care) Act 2000

The Children (Leaving Care) Act 2000 amends the Children Act 1989 so as to impose a duty on local authorities looking after children to advise, assist and befriend them with a view to promoting their welfare when they have ceased to look after them. The responsible local authority in each case has a duty to assess and meet the care and support needs of 'eligible' and 'relevant' children and young people and to assist 'former relevant' children, in particular, in respect of their employment, education and training.

An 'eligible' child is one aged 16–17 years who has been looked after by a local authority for 13 weeks (or periods amounting to that) which began after he reached the age of 14 years and ended after he reached the age of 16 years. A child does not come within the definition if the local authority has arranged to place him in a pre-planned series of short-term placements, none of which individually exceeds 4 weeks (even though they may amount in all to the prescribed period) and, at the end of each such placement, the child returns to the care of his parent, or of a person who is not a parent but who has parental responsibility for him: Schedule 2, paragraph 19B and the Children (Leaving Care) Regulations 2001.

In respect of an 'eligible' child, the authority must, in addition to its other duties to looked-after children, carry out an assessment of the child's needs with a view to determining what advice, assistance and support it would be appropriate for them to provide, while they are still looking after the child and after they have ceased to do so.

A 'relevant' child is one aged 16–17 years who is not being looked after by a local authority, but was, before last ceasing to be looked after, an 'eligible' child. A child who has returned home for a continuous period of 6 months is not to be treated as a relevant child unless the placement breaks down. In respect of a relevant child, the authority must:

- take reasonable steps to keep in touch;
- appoint a personal adviser;
- prepare a pathway plan;
- carry out an assessment of the child's needs with a view to determining what advice, assistance and support it would be appropriate to provide;
- safeguard and promote the child's welfare;
- unless satisfied that the child's welfare does not require it, support him by maintaining him or providing or maintaining him in suitable accommodation; and
- take reasonable steps to keep in touch with him, and, if contact is lost, immediately consider how to re-establish contact, take reasonable steps to do so and continue to take such steps until they succeed.

Duties to former relevant children

A 'former relevant' child is a person who has been a 'relevant' child (and still would be if he were under 18 years old) and a person who was being looked after by an authority when he attained the age of 18 years, and immediately before ceasing to be looked after was an 'eligible' child. In relation to such a child, the authority must take reasonable steps to keep in touch, and if it loses touch, must seek to re-establish contact. The authority must continue the appointment of a personal adviser and continue to keep the pathway plan under regular review. It must give a former relevant child assistance to the extent that the child's welfare and education or training needs require it. These duties subsist until the child reaches the age of 21 years, or until the end of a programme for education and training.

Persons qualifying for advice and assistance

A young person under 21 years old qualifies for advice and assistance if at any time after reaching the age of 16 years, but while still a child, he was (but is no longer) looked after, accommodated or fostered (whether privately or otherwise) by a local authority or a voluntary organisation, in a private children's home or in any accommodation provided (for at least 3 months) by an education authority, health authority, special health authority, local health board, primary care or national health service trust or in a care home or independent hospital. The responsible local authority is the one that last looked after the young person, wherever he is living in England or Wales. If he was not looked after by an authority, the authority where he resides is responsible.

The authority must take such steps as it thinks appropriate to contact the young person at such times as the authority thinks appropriate to discharge its duties. It must consider whether he needs help by way of advice or assistance. If he does, the authority must advise and befriend him if he was being looked after by a local authority or was accommodated by or on behalf of a voluntary organisation. If he was otherwise accommodated, the authority may advise and befriend him, and, in either case, may give assistance in kind or, exceptionally, in cash. It may give assistance by contributing to expenses incurred in living near the place where the young person qualifying for advice is employed or seeking employment, and may make a grant to meet expenses connected with his education or training. The duties apply to a person under 24 years old. If the person proposes to live, or is living, in the area of another local authority, the first local authority must inform the other authority about its responsibility.

Pathway plans

All eligible, relevant and former relevant children must have a pathway plan. The law now requires authorities to set out in it the advice, assistance and support that the authority intends to provide while looking after and when ceasing to look after each child. Each pathway plan must be maintained and reviewed until the young person is at least 21 years old, and longer if it is to cover education, training, career plans and support. Detailed provision about content is contained in the Children (Leaving Care) Regulations 2001. The pathway plan, which must be in writing and provided to the young person, must set out the manner in which the responsible authority proposes to meet the needs of the child, and the date by which, and by whom, any action required to implement any aspect of the plan will be carried out.

Personal adviser

All eligible, relevant and former relevant children must have a personal adviser, whose responsibility it is to help draw up the pathway plan. The adviser must ensure that the plan is implemented and developed as the young person's needs change. The adviser must keep in touch until the young person is 21 years old and ensure the provision of advice and support. Detailed duties are set out in the Children (Leaving Care) Regulations 2001.

Financial support

Relevant children and former relevant children are removed from entitlement to means-tested benefits. They remain the responsibility of the responsible local authority, which has to ensure that the vulnerable young people it looked after receive the care and help they need to grow into independence. Each local authority must continue to ensure that young people in and leaving care are suitably accommodated, supported and advised according to their needs.

Children's entitlement to mental health services

The Department of Health has issued detailed guidance concerning discharge from hospital in *Building Bridges: A Guide to Arrangements for Inter-agency Working for the Care and Management of Severely Mentally Ill People* (Department of Health, 1995e). This guidance was amended and updated in 1999 by *Effective Care Coordination in Mental Health Services* (Department of Health, 1999a).

After-care services: the Mental Health Act 1983

Section 117 of the Mental Health Act 1983 states: 'It shall be the duty of the Health Authority and of the local social services authority to provide, in cooperation with relevant voluntary agencies, after-care services for any person to whom this section applies until such time as the Health Authority and the local social services authority are satisfied that the person concerned is no longer in need of such services': s117(2). This section:

- applies only to patients detained under sections 3, 37, 47 or 48 of the Mental Health Act who then cease to be detained and (whether or not immediately after so ceasing) leave hospital: s117(1);
- requires the local health authority and the local social services authority to provide 'after-care'; and
- provides no definition for 'after-care', but, in the authors' opinion, this could include social support, day care arrangements and accommodation.

The care programme approach

The care programme approach (CPA) is a model for good practice in organising and managing community care. In England, the CPA 'requires health authorities, in collaboration with local authority social service departments to put in place specified arrangements for the care and treatment of mentally ill people in the community' (Department of Health, 1995e: 1.3.4).

The CPA has been policy in England for more than a decade, but until recently it did not apply in Wales, where a modified form of this approach was introduced in April 2003. In Wales, full implementation of the Welsh form of the CPA is required by the Welsh Assembly Government by December 2004. The intention is that services are:

- more accessible;
- more responsive to provide help and support quickly;
- enabled to seek out those who are difficult to engage;
- capable of involving users and carers in all aspects of planning; and
- effective in using care processes.

In 2002, the NHS in Wales and the Welsh Assembly Government published *Creating a Unified and Fair System for Accessing and Managing Care (UACM)*. The UACM Guidance (NHS Wales and Welsh Assembly Government, 2002) anticipated the future development of the CPA in Wales and its subsequent integration with the UACM system:

> 'The Welsh Assembly Government is committed to CPA being integrated with the Unified Assessment Process to provide a framework for care coordination in mental health care, with service users themselves providing the main focal point for care planning and delivery' (NHS Wales and Welsh Assembly Government, 2003).

The CPA policy for Wales is described in *Mental Health Policy Guidance* (NHS Wales and Welsh Assembly Government, 2003).

In England, the CPA has four main elements:

- systematic arrangements for assessing health and social care needs;
- formulation of a care plan to address these needs;
- appointment of a care coordinator to keep in touch with the patient;
- regular review: (Department of Health, 1995e: 1.3.5; amended Department of Health, 1999*a*).

Effective Care Coordination in Mental Health Services (Department of Health, 1999*a*) introduced some key changes to the CPA, including:

- a secondary service that combines health and social care;
- integration of the CPA with care management;
- two levels of the CPA – standard and enhanced; and
- a named care coordinator for each person on the CPA.

The original guidance was that the CPA in England was to apply to all in-patients about to be discharged from mental illness hospitals and all new patients accepted by specialist psychiatric services in England. However, now, it applies to everyone under the care of the secondary mental health services (health and social care), regardless of setting. Therefore, the CPA describes the approach that should be applied by specialist psychiatric services to the care plans for all service users aged 16 years or over.

Effective Care Coordination in Mental Health Services states that:

> 'The principles of the CPA are relevant to the care and treatment of younger and older people with mental health problems. The transition from child and adolescent services to adult services … is critical and must be managed effectively. Services should have in place clearly identified plans and protocols for meeting the needs of younger … people moving from one service to another' (Department of Health, 1999*a*: paragraph 17, p. 4).

In Wales, the CPA applies to all who come within the National Service Framework for adults of working age though 'the CPA principles also apply to those above the age of 65 and adolescents between 16 and 18 years of age who also meet the eligibility criteria ...' that are described in the guidance (NHS Wales and Welsh Assembly Government, 2003). As in England, the CPA in Wales has two levels; the standard CPA and the enhanced CPA. Similarly, the process requires the appointment of a care coordinator.

Compulsion in the community

At present, guardianship and supervised discharge orders are only available if the patient is aged 16 years or over. The purpose of guardianship is to enable patients to receive community care in circumstances in which it cannot be provided without the use of compulsory powers. (Code of practice, paragraph 13.1). The Mental Health (Patients in the Community) Act 1995 amended the Mental Health Act 1983 by introducing the power of 'after-care under supervision': s25A–J.

Guardianship and supervised discharge orders authorise social service or health professionals to require patients to:

- reside at a specified place;
- attend at places and at times so specified for the purpose of medical treatment, occupation, education or training;
- allow access to the patient to be given at any time, at any place where the patient is residing, to any doctor, ASW or other person so specified.

These powers are not 'community treatment orders' in that a patient subject to guardianship or supervised discharge cannot be compulsorily treated without their consent outside hospital. Even where and when it is necessary to administer treatment without consent to a patient who is 'liable to be detained' but on section 17 leave in the community, 'consideration should be given to recalling the patient to hospital' (Code of practice, paragraph 20.8).

A guardian has no power to take and convey the patient to any of the places the patient is required to be for medical treatment, occupation, education and training. However, if the patient is absent, without leave, from the place in which he or she resides, the patient may be taken into custody and returned to that place: Mental Health Act s18(3).

Once a patient becomes the subject of a supervised discharge order, the supervisor has the power to 'take and convey' the patient to 'any place where the patient is required to reside or to attend for the purpose of medical treatment, occupation, education or training': s25D(4) of the Mental Health Act 1983.

12
Wardship and the inherent jurisdiction of the High Court

Private law

The Children Act 1989 has no specific effect on private law wardship, save that the availability of section 8 orders has reduced its use.

Public law

In the public law field, the changes consequent on the Children Act 1989 are considerable. They include the following:

Section 100(1) and (2) provides that there can be no committal to care or supervision under the Family Law Reform Act 1969 section 7 or under the inherent jurisdiction of the High Court. Section 31 must be used.

The court has no power to require a local authority to accommodate a child and no power to confer on a local authority the power to determine any aspect of parental responsibility: s100(2)(b) and (d).

No child who is the subject of a care order may be made a ward of court: s100(2)(c). This means that local authorities, working with parents, are responsible for exercising parental responsibility for children in care, and do not seek guidance from or become subject to review by the court in difficult cases.

Nonetheless, a local authority may, with the consent of the High Court, apply for the exercise of that court's inherent jurisdiction, if the result it wishes to achieve cannot be achieved by any other means and if there is reason to believe that the child is likely to suffer significant harm if the jurisdiction is not exercised: s100(4) and (5). This might arise in cases that concern an application to override a child's or young person's refusal to consent to medical treatment where no other consent is available (see *Re R (A Minor) (Wardship: Medical Treatment)* [1992] Fam 11). It might also arise in the instance of injunctions to prevent invasion of a child's privacy, sterilisation, abortion, and any other matters not covered by section 8.

Effects of wardship and the inherent jurisdiction of the High Court

It is important to note the difference between the effects of wardship and the exercise of the inherent jurisdiction of the High Court.

The effects of wardship, in which the court is responsible for all important decisions concerning the child and which remains available where the child is not in care, are immediate once an application is made. Exercise of the High Court's inherent jurisdiction has no effect until there is a court order.

13 Special educational needs

Under the Education Act 1996, local education authorities, and funding authorities for grant-maintained schools, must have regard to the need to ensure that special provision is made for pupils with special educational needs.

Definition

Children have special educational needs if they have a learning difficulty. This means that they:

- have significantly greater difficulty in learning than the majority of children of the same age; or
- have a disability that either prevents or hinders them from making use of educational facilities of a kind provided for children of the same age in schools within the area of the local education authority; or
- are under 5 years old and fall within either of the above categories, or would do so if the special educational provision were not made for the child.

Duties to young people with special educational needs

The Education Act 1996 sets out duties to identify, assess and provide for children and young people with special educational needs. This may involve a multi-disciplinary assessment in consultation with parents. Mental health professionals may be involved at any stage of the process in advising, assessing or giving evidence.

The Education Act 1996 has a requirement for a Code of Practice of Special Educational Needs, which sets out detailed guidance. The latest version of that code was published in 2001 (Department for Education and Skills, 2001). It identifies a continuum of need extending from action within school to making a formal statement of special educational needs requiring specific provision of services.

Appeal

Parents have a right of appeal to the Special Educational Needs and Disability Discrimination Tribunal (SENDIST) against:

- a refusal to make an assessment;
- a decision not to make a statement;
- the content of a statement;
- a refusal to reassess a child with a statement.

Since 1 September 2002, the SENDIST has had powers to affect the practice of local education authorities and schools, if they are found to have discriminated against children with a disability.

14 Complaints procedures

A range of complaints procedures is available under the various Acts, with the consequent risk of duplication.

Children Act 1989

Children being looked after by a local authority, accommodated on behalf of a local authority by a voluntary organisation or otherwise accommodated in a registered children's home are entitled to use the complaints procedure required by section 26 of the Children Act 1989 and established in accordance with the Representations Procedure (Children) Regulations 1991.

Under sections 24D and 26 of the Children Act, local authorities must establish and publicise their procedures for considering any representations or complaints. This includes complaints made by:

- a child who they are looking after, or who is not being looked after but is in need;
- a person who qualifies for advice and assistance under section 24 (having been looked after);
- a 'relevant' or 'former relevant' child (see Chapter 11) and a person to whom they may contribute expenses or make a grant in respect of education or training;
- a parent or other person with parental responsibility;
- any foster parent;
- such other person as the authority or voluntary organisation considers has a sufficient interest in the child's welfare to warrant representations being considered by them about the discharge by the authority or voluntary organisation of any of their functions under Part III in relation to the child.

The procedure must ensure that at least one person who is not a member or officer of the authority takes part in the consideration of the complaint alongside any discussions conducted by the authority about the action to be taken in relation to the child in the light of the complaint.

The authority must have due regard to the findings of those considering the representation and must notify the child, the person making the representation and other affected persons of its reasons for its decision and of any action taken or to be taken. Although the decision about the child remains with the authority, if it ignores findings or fails to give any satisfactory reasons, it may be subject to judicial review.

Hospital Complaints Act 1985

Provision is made under the Hospital Complaints Act 1985 requiring hospitals to establish complaints procedures.

Mental Health Act 1983

The Code of Practice to the Mental Health Act 1989 states:

> 'Children and young people in hospital (both as informal and detained patients) and their parents or guardians should have ready access to existing complaints procedures, which should be drawn to their attention on their admission to hospital. The managers should appoint an officer whose responsibility it is to ensure that this is done and to assist any complainant': paragraph 30.13.

The Mental Health Act Commission (MHAC) also has the power to investigate complaints given by section 120(1) of the Mental Health Act 1983. This investigative power only exists in relation to detained patients. This power was created before the Hospital Complaints Act 1985 and the Children Act 1989 received Royal Assent. Thus, there are now several powers provided by these various Acts, with the consequent risk of duplication of proceedings. We suggest that would-be complainants should use the local procedures in the first instance, only invoking the MHAC process if they are not satisfied.

15
Work in the courts

There is a number of courts that deal with matters relating to children, and in which child and adolescent psychiatrists and a wide range of other professionals may, therefore, appear to give evidence of fact or as an expert.

The courts

Youth court

The youth court deals solely with juvenile offenders.

Magistrates' court

Under the Children Act 1989, a panel of magistrates has powers to deal with family proceedings in the family proceedings courts. The court may have a stipendiary magistrate, usually in urban areas, or more commonly a lay bench of two or three magistrates, sitting with a justices' clerk.

Magistrates do not have jurisdiction in relation to divorce, wardship and the inherent jurisdiction of the High Court, child abduction and some cases of domestic violence. They do have jurisdiction to make orders concerning children, including orders arising from powers given by Parts II, III and IV of the Children Act 1989 and those relating to maintenance, adoption and domestic violence between spouses.

County court

Children Act cases are also dealt with at a family hearing centre, a care centre, or the Principal Registry of the Family Division of the High Court, depending on the nature of the case. Care proceedings, allocated from the magistrates' court because of their complexity, are heard at a limited number of nationwide care centres by judges who have had special training for the purpose.

Applications relating to the wider range of orders available under the Children Act, and other matters such as residence and contact, divorce and nullity, domestic violence and adoption, can be heard at a family hearing centre.

High Court

Family matters are dealt with in the Family Division either at the Royal Courts of Justice in the Strand in London or at a district registry.

High Court judges or deputies sit alone to hear complex cases under the Children Act 1989. They also hear cases relating to adoption, wardship, the inherent jurisdiction and appeals from the magistrates' court. Certain appeals are to the Divisional Court, when two judges sit together.

Court of Appeal

Appeals from the High Court and county court go to the Court of Appeal and are heard by two or three Lords Justice of Appeal.

There is not always an automatic right of appeal and the leave of the judge may be necessary. Even where there is an automatic right, legal practitioners are warned not to pursue appeals without clear grounds for doing so.

House of Lords

The House of Lords is the final court of appeal in the United Kingdom and will only hear cases in which there is an issue of public importance. Cases are heard before five Law Lords.

Courts of Record

The High Court, Court of Appeal and the House of Lords are Courts of Record. Each can establish legal precedent, which is binding on courts lower than itself.

Evidence

Children Act 1989

The Children Act 1989 introduced some important changes relating to the evidence of children. The paragraphs that follow summarise the most substantial changes.

The evidence of a child witness in civil proceedings, who does not understand the nature of the oath, can be heard by the court if, in its opinion, the child understands that it is his duty to speak the truth and he has sufficient understanding to justify his evidence being heard: s96(2).

The Children (Admissibility of Hearsay Evidence) Order 1993 provides that hearsay evidence given in connection with the upbringing, maintenance or welfare of a child shall be admissible in family proceedings and child support proceedings in the magistrates' court. This also applies to civil proceedings in the county court and proceedings in the High Court.

Section 98 provides that, in care or protection proceedings, no person shall be excused from giving evidence, or answering any question on the ground that it may incriminate him or his spouse of an offence and that a statement or admission made shall not be admissible in criminal proceedings, other than those for perjury, against the person making the statement or his spouse.

Disclosing confidential information

Any person can be required by subpoena or witness summons to produce documents at court, notwithstanding that they may contain confidential information about a patient. In order to ensure that this information is available before the trial, it may be required by pre-trial order.

The House of Lords held, in *Re L (A Minor) (Police Investigation: Privilege)* [1997] AC 16, that the privilege attached to reports by third parties and prepared on the instructions of a client for the purposes of litigation relating to the children could be set aside. This was held to be distinct from legal professional privilege attaching to communications between a solicitor and a client which should be absolute. The court has discretion not to order disclosure, and may decline to do so, especially in the interests of a child.

The court may give permission for the disclosure of statements made in care proceedings for the purpose of investigation of allegations of a crime and for the disclosure of reports prepared at the request of parents for those proceedings: *Re EC (Disclosure of Material)* [1996] 2 FLR 725.

There is some uncertainty over the power of the court to override professional privilege and order disclosure of medical reports where the identity of the author of the report or the source of the reports is not known. The most favoured view at present is that set out by Mr Justice Thorpe in *Essex County Council v. R (Legal Professional Privilege)* [1993] 2 FLR 826. He held that legal representatives having reports relevant to the determination of a matter concerning children, but, contrary to the interests of their client, had a positive duty to disclose the reports to all the parties and to the courts. This view has been challenged in *S County Council v. B* [2000] 1 FCR 536, in which it was held that reports prepared for the purpose of other proceedings were privileged.

Expert evidence

Responding to requests for advice and evidence

The authors recommend that, in all cases, health care professionals should distinguish between providing professional information and advice and expert evidence.

For example, applications to the court under section 31 of the Children Act for a care or supervision order or for a secure accommodation order under section 25 are likely to require expert evidence. Frequently, this relates to the health or development of the child or the capabilities and alleged actions of a proposed carer, and is particularly relevant to the question as to whether a child is suffering or is likely to suffer significant harm.

In such circumstances, mental health practitioners can find that their expertise is sought by a number of individuals and organisations, such as:

- the local authority;
- the children's guardian;
- a member of the child's family.

In the experience of the authors, initial referrals in situations of this kind may not be entirely clear about what is required and the status of the advice requested. For example, local authorities may request both psychiatric or psycholgical assessment of a child for medico-legal purposes and also their continuing care and treatment. Also, in other circumstances, referral for routine assessment and professional intervention may be made, but it is not uncommon for health care professionals to be asked later to provide, for the authority's use in court, an account of their findings and the care that they have provided and that which they recommend for the future.

A third circumstance concerns children with whom a practitioner has had a professional relationship after an ordinary referral, but about whom the practitioner comes to have concerns that may require consideration of a statutory remedy. This might require reports to be prepared, if the statutory direction is pursued.

The authors distinguish providing 'professional' evidence on the basis of these three kinds of professional relationship (in which the child was and/or is the health care practitioner's principal client in the past or continuing from the present into the future) from providing expert evidence. Generally, expert witnesses are appointed by court order, usually with the agreement of the parties, in relationship to certain questions on which advice may be required.

In summary, where a local authority is requesting advice, a health care practitioner may have been involved before legal proceedings are initiated, but may need to continue this involvement afterwards. Otherwise, it is probable that expert advice will be sought specifically for the purpose of the proceedings. Therefore, it is important that health care practitioners should obtain clear instructions in all cases in which they envisage a medico-legal component as to:

- what is the overall context of the case;
- the purpose of the request for advice;

- the status of the request and on whose behalf it is made;
- the nature and type of any legal proceedings in hand or that could arise;
- the identity of any court or legal practitioners that are involved;
- the status that the practitioner will have before the courts (e.g. witness as to fact, 'professional' witness or 'expert witness');
- the existence or otherwise of an order for the practitioner to undertake the expert work (ordinarily, according to judges' rules, courts should not make orders for preparation of expert reports without the agreement of the identified expert);
- whether or not the child or any of the children involved is a ward of court (as particular restrictions apply to examination of them and provision of opinions about them by psychiatrists and psychologists);
- what questions are to be considered;
- the anticipated volume, style and duration of the work requested;
- the nature of any report required and the date by which it should be filed with the court;
- the source of funding to pay for the work to be done; and
- agreement that any report will be shared by all parties.

Further guidance on this aspect of the work can be found in *Child Psychiatry and the Law* (Black *et al*, 1998).

Roles of experts

The courts have held that experts must only express opinions that they genuinely hold and that are not biased in favour of one party. If an expert does seek to promote a particular case, the report must make that clear, but that approach should be avoided. A misleading opinion may well inhibit a proper assessment of the case by non-medical professional advisers; it may increase costs and lead parties (in particular, parents) to false views and hopes.

A helpful summary of the duties of an expert giving evidence is set out in *Re AB (A Minor) (Medical Issues)* [1995] 1 FLR 181 and is extracted below.

- Expert evidence presented to the court should be (and should be seen to be) the independent product of the expert, uninfluenced as to form or content by the exigencies of litigation.
- An expert witness should provide independent assistance to the court by way of objective, unbiased opinion in relation to matters within his expertise.
- An expert witness should never assume the role of advocate.
- An expert witness should state the facts or assumptions on which his opinion is based. He should not omit to consider material facts which detract from his concluded opinion.
- An expert witness should make it clear when a particular question falls outside his expertise.
- If an expert's opinion is not properly researched because he considers that insufficient data are available, then this must be stated with an indication that the opinion is no more than a provisional one.

- If after exchange of reports, an expert witness changes his view on a material matter, such change of view should be communicated to the other side without delay and, when appropriate, to the court.
- Where expert evidence refers to photographs, reports or other similar documents, they must be provided to the opposite party at the same time as the exchange of reports.

There is increasing pressure on experts to discuss reports with each other prior to the hearing, in an attempt to reach agreement or limit the issues: *Re M (Minors) (Care Proceedings: Child's Wishes)* [1994] 1 FLR 749. Directions should be given by the court to ensure that sufficient time is set aside for expert evidence: *Re MD and TD (Minors) (Time Estimates)* [1994] 2 FLR 336. The parties and the court should have an understanding of the issues involved at any directions hearing.

The requirements of the Lord Chancellor's Department (now the Department for Constitutional Affairs)

In June 2003, the Lord Chancellor's Department (now the Department for Constitutional Affairs) issued the Protocol for Judicial Case Management in Public Law Children Act Cases. It has within it, as Appendix C, a Code of Practice for Expert Witnesses in Family Proceedings.

The intention of that Code is to provide the court with early information to enable it to determine whether it is necessary and/or applicable to ask an expert to assist the court in cases where appointment of an expert is being considered.

Although this Code is, for the most part, laid out as a series of requirements on the solicitors for the parties to public law proceedings who propose to instruct an expert, it also lists, directly and by implication, requirements and actions that now fall on experts at each stage from preliminary enquiries of experts through to post-hearing action. In particular, it covers:

- the duties of experts;
- preparation;
- letters of instruction;
- the expert's report;
- experts' discussion;
- attending court; and
- post-hearing action.

The Code clearly states that an expert in family proceedings has an overriding duty to the court that takes precedence over any obligation to the person from whom he or she has received instructions or by whom he or she is paid. Thus, the requirements of the Code echo much of our advice in this chapter and we strongly recommend that readers consult that appendix, as it is now the authoritative source relating to the conduct of experts in public law cases in England and Wales.

Credibility of expert witnesses

The question concerning whether an expert witness can give evidence to a court about whether a child is telling the truth has produced different responses from the Court of Appeal. At the time of concluding this second edition, the cumulative effect of decisions in *Re N (A Minor) (Child Abuse: Evidence)* [1996] 2 FLR 214, CA and *Re M and R (Minors)* [1996] 2 FLR 195, CA, is as follows:

- An expert witness may give evidence about whether a child is telling the truth, but the relevance of that evidence and the weight to be attached to it is a matter for the judge.
- If a video recording of the evidence of a child is admitted as a form of hearsay evidence, it is for the judge to decide its weight and credibility. He should judge the internal consistency and inconsistency of the story. He should look for any inherent improbabilities in the truth of what the child has related and should decide what part, if any, he could believe.
- The judge should receive expert evidence to explain and interpret the video recording. This should cover such things as the nuances of emotion and behaviour, the gestures and the body movements, the use or non-use of language and its imagery, the vocal inflections and intonations, the pace and pressure of the interview, the child's intellectual and verbal abilities (or lack of them) and any signs (or absence of signs) of fantasising.
- It is for the judge to separate admissible from inadmissible expert evidence. Evidence from an expert might best be couched in terms that a particular fact is consistent or inconsistent with sexual abuse, for example, and that it renders the child's evidence capable or incapable of being accepted by the judge as true.
- Evidence of a diagnosis of sexual abuse calls for a very high level of expertise. For the court to rely on opinion as evidence, even to admit it, the qualifications of the witness must extend beyond experience gained as a social worker and require clinical experience as or akin to a child psychologist or child psychiatrist.

Funding

It is important to establish the basis for funding the work of an expert witness. If expert advice is sought by a local authority, in or out of court, the expert should establish whether work is expected to be done under any contract he or she may have with the National Health Service (NHS) or by separate payment. We consider that it is more likely that the NHS acquires such a responsibility in the three instances described on page 104, in which the practitioners are asked for their 'professional opinion', rather than in respect of provision of expert opinion ordered by a court. Also, it is often the case that the experts who are appointed ordinarily work at a distance from the agency making the request.

If the request for an expert opinion comes from a children's guardian or a solicitor representing a member of the family, it is likely that financial arrangements will have to be made outside any NHS provision. Funding may be provided through the legal aid system.

Legal advice

It is important that all agencies and individual professionals involved in managing the mental health of children and young people should have ready access to good legal advice. These advisers should be familiar with both mental health and children's legislation.

In some cases, the mental health expert will only be an adviser to or witness in an action being taken by another agency. In those circumstances, the advice and guidance of their legal advisers may be sufficient. In other cases, the expert may need to have access to legal advice for the purposes of his own agency or if he is unsure about what he is being asked to do.

The availability of that expertise and the different professional perspective is an essential benefit to the provision of an appropriate service. Knowledge and understanding of the legal framework should lead to better informed decision-making on policy and on individual cases. Ultimately, better all-round understanding should enable improvements in the legal system itself to be brought about.

Further reading

Despite the number of explanatory texts available, the Children Act 1989, as amended, along with Regulations and Orders issued by the Secretaries of State and now the devolved administration in Wales in pursuance of their duties remain the only truly authoritative source of information on what is or is not lawful in relation to children. Rules of court are contained in a number of orders by the Lord Chancellor's Department (1991*a–c*).

Similarly, the Mental Health Act 1983 is the essential source of mental health law. The Code of Practice for the Mental Health Act 1983 has been referred to in various chapters in this book. The updated current version of the Code was laid before Parliament on 3 December 1998 and came into force on 1 April 1999.

In 1991, Her Majesty's Stationery Office (HMSO), now The Stationery Office, published detailed guidance and regulations on the Children Act 1989 in nine volumes:

Volume 1 *Court Orders*

Volume 2 *Family Support, Day Care and Education Provision for Young Children*

Volume 3 *Family Placements*

Volume 4 *Residential Care*

Volume 5 *Independent Schools*

Volume 6 *Children with Disabilities*

Volume 7 *Guardians Ad Litem and Court Processes*

Volume 8 *Private Fostering and Miscellaneous*

Volume 9 *Adoption Issues*

They give authoritative guidance about the intentions and requirements of the Children Act 1989 and generate a comprehensive picture of its impact on professional practice.

A series of books on the Children Act have been published. For example, *The Children Act 1989 in Practice* (White *et al*, 2002) contains a commentary on the main provisions and reproduces the Act, as amended, in full. Various training packs have been produced by statutory, voluntary and educational bodies, including the Open University, the National Children's Bureau and the Department of Health.

Additionally, the former National Health Service (NHS) Health Advisory Service published a number of texts of direct relevance to commissioning and providing mental health services for children and adolescents. These are:

Suicide Prevention – The Challenge Confronted (ISBN 011 321821 4). London: HMSO, 1994.

Together We Stand – The Commissioning, Role and Management of Child and Adolescent Mental Health Services (ISBN 011 321904 0). London: HMSO, 1995.

A Place in Mind – Commissioning and Providing Mental Health Services for People Who Are Homeless (ISBN 011 321925 3). London: HMSO, 1995.

The Substance of Young Needs – Commissioning and Providing Services for Children and Adolescents Who Use and Misuse Substances (ISBN 0 11 321934 2). London: HMSO, 1996.

Recently, three books have been published that are useful soruces of direct advice to practitioners and of indirect or implied advice to service designers, commissioners and managers. They are:

Communicating with Vulnerable Children: A Guide for Practitioners. By D. P. H. Jones (ISBN 1 901242 91 9). London: Gaskell, 2003.

Child and Adolescent Mental Health Services: An Operational Handbook. Edited by G. Richardson & I. Partridge (ISBN 1 901242 96 X). London: Gaskell, 2003.

Young People and Substance Misuse. Edited by I. Crome, H. Ghodse, E. Gilvarry & P. McArdle (ISBN 0 904671 01 2). London: Gaskell, 2004.

Each of these books reports on the challenges facing services and on their capacities and capabilities at the point that each was written. In our opinion, both the challenges they describe and much of the advice they offer are still relevant now. Each advises on good practice in commissioning and delivering services and recommends ways in which that good practice can be implemented. Also, the constraints, challenges, duties and enabling powers, as framed by the law at the time of publication, are considered, as are ways, which remain appropriate, of putting good practice into effect within a lawful framework.

The bibliography on pages 111–114 provides a list of reports, books and government policy that readers may find helpful. Some of these sources are referred to in this book. Others are provided as more general reading for those people who wish to look more deeply into the policy and legislative frameworks that relate to children's welfare, care and treatment.

Websites

The following organisations are further sources of information and advice:

- Centre for Evidence-Based Mental Health: www.cebmh.com
- Mind: www.mind.org.uk
- Royal College of Psychiatrists: www.rcpsych.ac.uk
- Sainsbury Centre for Mental Health: www.scmh.org.uk
- Stationery Office: www.official-documents.co.uk

Bibliography

Adcock, M., White, R. & Hollows, A. (eds) (1998) *Significant Harm: Its Management and Outcome* (2nd edn). Croydon: Significant Publications.

Aldgate, J. & Statham, J. (2001) *The Children Act Now: Messages from Research*. London: Stationery Office.

Ashford, M. & Chard, A. (1999) *Defending Young People*. London: Legal Action Group.

Bailey, S. & Harbour, A. (1999) The law and a child's consent to treatment (England and Wales). *Child Psychology and Psychiatry Review*, **4**, 30–34.

Bartlett, P. & Sandland, R. (2003) *Mental Health Law – Policy and Practice*. Oxford: Oxford University Press.

Black, D., Harris Hendriks, J. & Wolkind, S. (eds) (1998) *Child Psychiatry and the Law* (3rd edn). London: Gaskell.

British Medical Association (2001) *Consent, Rights and Choices in Health Care for Children and Young People.* London: BMJ Books.

British Medical Association & Law Society (1995) *Assessment of Mental Capacity – Guidance for Doctors and Lawyers*. London: BMA.

Clements, L. (2000) *Community Care and the Law*. London: Legal Action Group.

Crome, I., Ghodse, H., Gilvarry, E., *et al* (eds) (2004) *Young People and Substance Misuse*. London: Gaskell.

Department for Education and Skills (2001) *Statutory Instrument 2001 No. 3943 (C.135) The Education (Special Educational Needs Code of Practice) (Appointed Day) (England) Order 2001*. London: Stationery Office. http://www.hmso.gov.uk/si/si2001/20013943.htm

Department of Health (1990) *The Care Programme Approach*. HC(90)28/LASSL(90)11. London: HMSO.

Department of Health (1991*a*) *Guidance and Regulations on the Children Act 1989*: vol. 1, *Court Orders*; vol. 2, *Family Support, Day Care and Education Provision for Young Children*; vol. 3, *Family Placements*; vol. 4 *Residential Care*; vol. 5 *Independent Schools*; vol. 6, *Children with Disabilities*; vol. 7, *Guardians Ad Litem and Court Processes*; vol. 8, *Private Fostering and Miscellaneous*; vol. 9, *Adoption Issues*. London: HMSO.

Department of Health (1991*b*) *Welfare of Children and Young People in Hospital*. London: HMSO.

Department of Health (1991*c*) *The Care of Children – Principles and Practice in Regulations and Guidance*. London: HMSO.

Department of Health (1991*d*) *The Children Act 1989 – An Introductory Guide for the NHS*. London: HMSO.

Department of Health (1991e) *Patterns and Outcomes in Child Placement: Messages from Research and their Implications*. London: HMSO.

Department of Health (1993) *Guidance on Permissible Forms of Control in Residential Care*. London: HMSO.

Department of Health (1995*a*) *Child Protection – The Challenge of Partnership in Child Protection: Practice Guide*. London: HMSO.

Department of Health (1995*b*) *Child Protection: Messages from Research*. London: HMSO.

Department of Health (1995c) *Child Protection: Clarification of Arrangements between the NHS and other Agencies*. London: HMSO.

Department of Health (1995*d*) *Child Protection: Medical Responsibilities*. London: HMSO.

Department of Health (1995*e*) *Building Bridges: A Guide to Arrangements for Inter-Agency Working for the Care and Protection of Severely Mentally Ill People.* London: Department of Health.

Department of Health (1996) *Guidance on Supervised Discharge (After-care under Supervision) and Related Provisions.* London: Department of Health.

Department of Health (1999*a*) *Effective Care Coordination in Mental Health Services. Modernising the Care Programme Approach.* London: Department of Health.

Department of Health (1999*b*) *Report of the Expert Committee. Review of the Mental Health Act 1983*. London: Stationery Office.

Department of Health (2000*a*) *Framework for the Assessment of Children in Need and their Families.* London: Stationery Office.

Department of Health (2000*b*) *Assessing Children in Need and Their Families: Practice Guidance.* London: Stationery Office.

Department of Health (2001*a*) *The Mental Health Act 1983 Guidance for General Practitioners: Medical Examinations and Medical Recommendations Under The Act.* London: Department of Health.

Department of Health (2001*b*) *Reference Guide to Consent for Examination or Treatment*. London: Department of Health.

Department of Health (2001c) *The Children Act Now: Messages from Research.* London: Stationery Office.

Department of Health (2002) *Safeguarding Children in Whom Illness is Fabricated or Induced*. London: Department of Health.

Department of Health & Welsh Office (1999) *Code of Practice, Mental Health Act 1983*. London: HMSO.

Department of Health, Home Office & Department for Education and Skills (1999) *Working Together to Safeguard Children: A Guide to Inter-Agency Working to Safeguard and Promote the Welfare of Children*. London: Stationery Office.

Eekelaar, J. & Dingwall, R. (1990) *The Reform of Child Care Law – A Practical Guide to the Children Act 1989*. London: Routledge.

Eldergill, A. (1997) *Mental Health Review Tribunals: Law and Practice.* London: Sweet & Maxwell.

Elton, A., Honig, P., Bentovim, A., *et al* (1995) Withholding consent to lifesaving treatments: three cases. *BMJ*, **310**, 373–377.

Family Courts Consortium (1991) *Information Pack and Bulletin*. London: FCC.

Fennell, P. (1996) *Treatment Without Consent: Law, Psychiatry and the Treatment of Mentally Disordered People since 1845*. London: Routledge.

Fortin, J. (2003) *Children's Rights and the Developing Law* (2nd edn) London: Butterworth.

Hendrick, J. (1993) *Child Care Law for Health Professionals*. Oxford: Radcliffe Medical Press.

Harris Hendriks, J. & Williams, R. (1992) The Children Act 1989 – England and Wales. *Journal of Child Psychology and Psychiatry*, **14**, 213–220.

Harris Hendriks, J., Richardson, G. & Williams, R. (1990) Ethical and legal issues. In *Child and Adolescent Psychiatry: Into the 1990s* (Occasional Paper OP8) (eds J. Harris Hendriks & D. Black), pp. 44–50. London: Royal College of Psychiatrists.

Hoggett, B. (1996) *Mental Health Law* (4th edn). London: Sweet & Maxwell.

Jones, D. P. H. (1991) Working with the Children Act: tasks and responsibilities of the child and adolescent psychiatrist. In *Proceedings of the Children Act 1989 Course* (Occasional Paper OP12), pp. 23–41. London: Royal College of Psychiatrists.

Jones, D. P. H. (2003) *Communicating with Vulnerable Children: A Guide for Practitioners.* London: Gaskell.

Jones, R. (2003) *Mental Health Act Manual* (8th edn) London: Thomson, Sweet & Maxwell.

Lord Chancellor's Department (various dates) *The Children Act Advisory Committee Reports, 1991–92, 1992–93, 1993–94, 1994–95 and 1995–96.* London: HMSO.

Lord Chancellor's Department (1991*a*) *Family Proceedings Rules 1991*. London: HMSO.

Lord Chancellor's Department (1991*b*) *Family Proceedings Courts (Children Act 1989) Rules 1991*. London: HMSO.

Lord Chancellor's Department (1991*c*) *Children (Allocation of Proceedings) Order 1991*. London: HMSO.

Lord Chancellor's Department (2003) *Protocol for Judicial Case Management in Public Law Children Act Cases*. London: Stationery Office.

Mears, A., White, R., Banerjee, S., *et al* (2001) *An Evaluation of the Use of the Children Act 1989 and the Mental Health Act 1983 in Children and Adolescents in Psychiatric Settings (CAMHA-CAPS).* London: Royal College of Psychiatrists' Research Unit.

Mental Health Act Commission (1999) *Mental Health Act Commission Guidance Note 3. Guidance on the Treatment of Anorexia Nervosa under the Mental Health Act 1983*. London: Stationery Office. http://www.mhac.trent.nhs.uk/anorexia.pdf

Mental Health Act Commission (2001) *Ninth Biennial Report 1999–2001*. London: Stationery Office.

Mental Health Act Commission (2003) *Tenth Biennial Report 2001–2003*. London: Stationery Office.

Montgomery, J. (2002) *Health Care Law* (2nd edn). Oxford: Oxford University Press.

National Assembly for Wales (2001*a*) *Working Together to Safeguard Children: A Guide for Inter-Agency Working to Safeguard and Promote the Welfare of Children*. London: Stationery Office.

National Assembly for Wales (2001*b*) *Framework for the Assessment of Children in Need and their Families.* London: Stationery Office.

National Assembly for Wales (2002) *Too Serious a Thing – The Review of Safeguards for Children and Young People Treated and Cared for by the NHS in Wales (The Carlile Review).* Cardiff: National Assembly for Wales.

National Children's Bureau (1989) *The Children Act 1989. Highlight No. 91*. London: NCB.

National Children's Bureau (1990) *Working with the Children Act 1989*. London: NCB.

NHS Management Executive (1990) *Guidance on Consent to Examination and Treatment*. London: Department of Health.

NHS Wales and Welsh Assembly Government (2002) *Creating a Unified and Fair System for Assessing and Managing Care (UACM)*. Cardiff: Welsh Assembly Government.

NHS Wales and Welsh Assembly Government (2003) *Mental Health Policy Guidance – The Care Programme Approach for Mental Health Service Users: A Unified and Fair System for Managing Care*. Cardiff: Welsh Assembly Government.

Open University (1991) *The Children Act 1989 – Putting it into Practice*. Milton Keynes: Open University.

Plotnikoff, J. & Woolfson, R. (1996) *Reporting to Court under the Children Act*: London: HMSO.

Read J & Clements L (2001) *Disabled Children and the Law*. London: Jessica Kingsley.

Richardson, G. & Partridge, I. (eds) (2003) *Child and Adolescent Mental Health Services: An Operational Handbook*. London: Gaskell.

Ruegger, M. (1994) Children's rights in relation to giving and withholding treatment. In *Children and the Law* (ed. D L Lockton), pp. 43–49. Leicester: De Montfort University Law School.

Scott, A., Shaw, M. & Joughin, C. (2001) *Finding the Evidence – A Gateway to the Literature in Child and Adolescent Mental Health* (2nd edn). London: Gaskell.

Spencer, J. R. & Flin, R. (1990) *The Evidence of Children*. London: Blackstone.

Starmer, K. (1999) *European Human Rights Law*. London: Legal Action Group.

Ward, R. (2001) *Young Offenders – Law, Practice and Procedure*. Bristol: Jordans.

White, R., Carr, P. & Lowe, N. (2002) *The Children Act 1989 in Practice* (3rd edn). London: Butterworth.

Williams, R. & Harris Hendriks, J. (1991) Introducing the Children Act 1989. *General Practitioner*, 18 October, 52–58.

Williams, R. & Harris Hendriks, J. (1992) Introducing the Children Act 1989. In *The Law and General Practice* (ed. D. Pickersgill). Oxford: Radcliffe Medical Press.

Williams, R. & Salmon, G. (2002) Collaboration in commissioning and delivering child and adolescent mental health services. *Current Opinion in Psychiatry*, **15**, 349–353.

Index

Legal cases index

(page numbers are shown in *italic*, for clarity)

Subject index